TETRALOGY 1
A Book of Bard
(Cantus-Dose-Syzygy-Shadow Catching)

Brad Dehler

TROIKA STUDIOS & PUBLISHNG
SALEM, OREGON

0

*

Tetralogy 1: A Book of Bard

Copyright © Brad Dehler 2025

ALL RIGHTS RESERVED. No part of this work covered by the copyright herein may be reproduced, transmitted, stored, or used in any form or by any means graphic, electronic, or mechanical, including but not limited to photocopying, recording, scanning, digitizing, taping, Web distribution, information networks, or information storage and retrieval systems, except as permitted under Section 107 or 108 of the 1976 United States Copyright Act, without the prior written permission of the author.

Printed in the United States of America
1st Edition

Additional copies are available at
Barnes and Noble // Books-A-Million
Booktopia.com.au // Ebay // Thriftbooks
Abebooks.com // Goodreads.com // WritersCafe
Betterworldbooks.com // Duckscottage.com
or www.Amazon.com

For product information, permission to use material from
this text, or further permissions questions- please e-mail to:
Troika7@gmail.com

A special thanks to the formatters at CreateSpace
and to the details, content, and quality reviewers from Kindle Direct Publishing KDP
A Book of Bard; Poemadeh candidate

ISBN-13: 978-1-966716-06-8 & ISBN-10: 1-966716-06-0
Hardcover ISBN: 978-1-966716-07-5

Troika Studios & Publishng; Salem, Oregon
Printing by KDP/CreateSpace; Charlotte, South Carolina
An Amazon Company
USA

*

CANTUS

2nd Edition (5in x 8in)
ISBN 13: 978-1-966716-00-6 ◘ *ISBN 10: 1-966716-00-1*
Troika Studios & Publishng
Copyright © Brad Dehler 2010, 2025

Table of Contents

Black Crow	6
In Quitting	7
Delving Deeper	8
I Know We Defame	9
She Fills	10
Life Is	11
Spontaneous	12
At This Address	13
In The Desert	14
Your Limitations	15
Dismiss	16
Embrace	17
Innundate You	18
Everyone Has Holes	19
Practice	20
The Counselor Should	21
Mankind	22
Hell Has Firelight	23
In Reference	24
Change Within Me	25
Virtue	26
Enemies Introduce	27
Understand Emptiness	28
Seed	29
Chased Illusion	30
Walked The Lengths	31
Ounce Of Anger	32

Throw Things To The Sky	33
Wise Man	34
Ability Falls To Will	35
Mad At My Size	36
Be Strong	37
Just This Recent	38
Vision Impaired	39
You Can't Walk	40
Fifty Years	41
I Stumble	42
Agony	43
Lost Warmth	44
Hark	45
How Coarse	46
To Improve	47
Fires To Extinguish	48
Bones Of The Young	49
Dead On Arrival	50
Woe To Thee	51
Wrought Tears	52
Truth Is Right	53
Progressive Thought	54
The Intelligence Of The World	55
Shadow Catcher	56
Under The Wreckage	57
My Shadow Takes A Stance	58
Curse Not	59
The Past Is Gone	60
Obedient Student	61
The Unconcerned	62
In Due Time	63
Reach High	64
We Are So Prone	65
I Have Been Down (These Streets)	66
Our Predator	67

Of Fortune and Struggle	68
Measure of Conviction	69
With This Designation	70
Simmer Simmer	71
Plots Granted	72
Early on I Discovered	73
Stumbled Upon a Stool	74
The Most Robust Rat	75
The Eternal Chases Me	76
Ethereal Promises	77
Be Like the Fire	78
Have Slight Faith	79
Be It Darkness or Bright	80
Buffalo Hunt	81
Madness Abounds	82
Postcard From Vedder	83
I End Up Ahead	84
A Good Heart Objects	85
Able to Bestow	86
Coach Called	87
Deficiency of Student	88
What is Left	89
Our Second Day of School	90
Into Misuse	91
The Sky is Blue	92
Pursuant of that Feeling	93
The Line Between	94
There is a Man	95
In Exhaustion	96
Lessons in Love	97
What is Longer?	98
Baptised by the Cemetery	99
Of Something Great	100
Color Spectrum	101
Diverting My Eyes	102

Dark Day of Pain	103
In Experience and Contemplation	104
Figures in the Distance	105
People Are Looking	106
Prudent Purveyor	107
My Weaknesses	108
Know it by Heart	109
I Read an Acclaimed Book	110
Revelation	111
Quack Doctor	112
Among Those Hours	113
This World Without Me	114
We Chased the Titles	115
The Counterbalance	116
When Depleted	117
Current Trajectory	118
Drop in the Ocean	119
Tattered Bounties	120
To Appoint	121
Loss of Sight	122
Economic Seer	123
One's Body Grows	124
Up Top a Crow's Nest	125
All Ideas	126
Dispel Your Beliefs	127
So Irrelevant	128
Not Enough to be Human	129
Once the Noise Drops	130
Landed on a Syzygy	131
We are a World of Wars	132
To the Prose	133
Ever Afterglow	134-137

*

Black crow
Blue night
Caw
Gawk
Flock…
    Less
Flies in circles

                    Vacaville, CA 1993

*

In quitting,
        One lays one's power down
        To weakness
The power exists
But the weak
        Have lost recognition

                          Salem 11.06.08

*

Delving deeper into one's self
    Polarizes
The depths of one's self
    Determine the righteousness
    Of such an act

                  Corvallis, OR 12.09.08

*

I know we defame
        What we do not understand
In absentia
But I am here
        And I am clear
It is not of good use

                        Salem 02.28.07

*

She fills
    Every sense in every word
Dedicated to the one I love:
    Johanna
Dedicated to Johanna
    The one I love
To Johanna
The Johanna
One- Johanna
Dedicated to the Johanna I love
Dedicated to the one,
    Johanna, Love
Love Johanna
    My love is Johanna
Dedicated to the one I Johanna
I- Johanna
One.

                        Salem 03.09.01 @1027

*

Life is a lesson
    In how to learn

                      Corvallis, OR 1999

*

Spontaneous reaction
    Kills the messenger

*

At this address no more
At one time parenting
      To raise this daughter
      To culpability
To protect her
      But allow struggle
      To teach
His dynasty remains in her blue eyes
And her quiet peace

*

In the desert,
    The parched sand
Indicative of my throat
In the forest,
    Moisture pooled on my tongue-
    Akin to the leaves
The sea...
    The sea deceived me

*

Your limitations-
    Your cross
But your attitude
    Is your crucifixion

*

Dismiss all knowledge
   By accepting all beliefs

*

Embrace others' deficiencies
    To handicap yourself with excuse
Reformulate oxymoron
    Into reciprocal terms
Avoiding answers
Fornicating with contentment
Recluse- to hide and never seek
    Prove me wrong
    Prove anything right
In guise of a prophet

*

Inundate you with love
For by a chance moment
Regressed
A moment remiss

*

Everyone
        Has holes in their thinking
Evermore in their speaking
Our dubious task is
        To not fall inside

Practice as if
      An underdog
Play as
      The champion

                              Salem 03.20.06

*

The counselor should be architect
Collaborating with the client,
    The construction worker
Erroneous for the counselor
To interfere
    As the construction worker
Turning the client into
    The inanimate project

                            Salem 06.27.06

*

Mankind is full of desire
What are we, if not loyal?
New desire breeds of
    New mutiny

                                         Portland, OR 06.30.09

*

One exclaims,
    'Tonight is not as dark as last night'
The other glibs,
    'Even Hell has firelight'
Some are afraid
    Of another's cognition
But I say,
    How many are afraid of their own?

                        Portland, OR 05.31.09

*

Whether in reference
    Of behind, or
      In front of
The sun
We are speaking
    Geocentrically

                            Portland, OR 06.25.09

*

There was change within me
    When I was with you
But there was no change within you,
    When with me
I rose and
    Conceived of things
While you allowed things
    Contrive you

                                         Portland, OR 06.02.09

*

Virtue-
    None sought
Your advice-
    Dead to me
Your efforts-
    An epitaph

                    Portland, OR 07.11.09

*

Enemies introduce anger
    Inside you
There it dwells
    And is used
To destroy you

                      Portland, OR 07.06.09

*

To understand emptying
To understand humility
    We cannot visit once
But visit again and again
To learn
    Again and again

                      Portland, OR 07.06.09

*

You may plant or eat
　　The seed
Depending on the urgency
　　Of need

　　　　　　　　　　　　Salem 03.21.06

Chased illusion
      So long
It became delusion
When can we ever
      Be for certain
We move by whim

*

I have walked the lengths
      Of bohemia
      And Sparta
Found the middle ground
More profound

*

With an ounce of anger
And pound of retribution
You are unsatisfied
Such things still
      Weigh on you

*

How many times we throw things
        To the sky
Forgetting the fallout
The highest
        One can throw
        With any given effort
Is directly up
So it returns
        Upon our head

The wise man
        Has much to learn
The fool
        Is full of knowledge

*

Ability falls to will
It matters not of the examination
    But of the heart-
    Examine it
I care
    But can't obsess
I do
    But don't excess
Got a little piece of Heaven
    But can't explain

                                      Fairfield, CA 1994

*

Mad at my size
Mole hills eventuate
    Into mountains
This is the Truth as I see it
    And if unfettered- my sight
This is Truth
I refer to blindness
    Not in physical terms
For the sightlessness
    Is not the blind man's burden
Inclined to insight
Our obligations staggering
    Studied from afar

                                    Corvallis, OR 03.28.01

*

Be strong in wretchedness
Not assured in righteousness
Nor defeated
There is a path
    In which we are all called
Listen
    Or defeat will meet you soundly

                Covington, LA 06.27.04

Just this, recent
    I realize the hollowness is not permanent
In this
    I weigh my vision
    To the void
Tired from the pain
Not to fill a hole
    But fulfill my soul
My all journeys with you
Our journey onward
    Three rosebuds
Fallen and caught
    Catchers do keep
Given
    Each other
In love
    We reap
Kiss the womb
    Of great potential
Eye to eye
    With the woman
    Who delivers me
It is the first time
    Another has seen
    My innate marvels
I see you too
And how adored
    Is that translation
    Whispered back
Time to time
    We must part
    From our embrace
Until when?
Realize a difference
    Between here and Heaven

*

Vision impaired to
    The ruins we knew
Doubtful due to
    Truths we misconstrue
I hoped you wouldn't forget
    The tomb
I hoped you wouldn't forget
    My company
In the big wide plain
    Things look all alone
Stay by my side
    I will show you home
Understand now
    So one can love now
It's the dust that
    Shows your past
It's your waste that
    Attracts the rats
My swollen feet mock surprise
Seldom surprised
    Always appalled
Journey for cure
    Healed along the way

                        Fairfield, CA 09.02.96

*

You can't walk where
    He did walk
He can't sing when
    You did
You couldn't believe
    You were shown up
    By just one kid
Watches oceans crumble
    By his feet
Waits 'til blue sky turns black
Suddenly he isn't so big
Suddenly he isn't so
Salt water swells
    To the knees
The tide pulls out
    Sky turns red
The tide will bring me
    Back again
Like it always does

*

Fifty years before my first
Were my precious words preceded?
    Dwindle I to apathy accursed
These words of diction
    Beset so long ago
These doubts silence thought
    Never to reach modern minds
    Lay to rot, negate conviction
All goodness need renew
If seek you, truth
    Then seek, renew
Love is but dead
    Without each day, a resurrection

        Salem 08.04.09 @0302

*

I stumble
    Weak and weary
A blade that lost its edge
Grind to sharpen
By the profession of thinking clearly
Id is in the rats in the race
66 channels
    Nothing is on
66 newspapers
    One opinion
Explain the inane reasoning
I bleed much more
    When I know I should not have
    Taken the chance
And so I
    Feel unwelcome in my room
Keep the pilot light lit
    Come tomorrow
Come tomorrow
Not to the know the
    How or when

        Corvallis, OR 10.22.98 @1000

*

The converse of wretched agony
    Is not ecstasy
It is
    Righteous suffering

                    Albany, OR 09.28.03

*

Hand has lost warmth
    Bundle now in this season
In my earlier time
    I saw spontaneous joy
Free- open
Time was intoxicated
Feel this pain
    I am alive
Absorb this rain
    I will survive

                               Fairfield, CA 1996

*

Oh, hark!
    A mark of incense
Oh, hark!
    A spot of light
Raised, my dermis
Tasted, blood
Chiming of bells
    Pay the toll
    I cross the bejeweled bridge
Echoes reverberate in my chest
I smell the candles burning
And then
    Ingestion consumes my rest

                      Albany, OR 10.12.03

*

How coarse
    Those tender lips
How bitter
    Those sweet nothings
Deceptive intent
    Sways the literal
Disdain stays both hearts

                                  Salem 02.04.08

*

To improve upon the young,
    Slow them
    Into contemplation
To improve upon the old,
    Hasten them
    Into desire
All are afflicted
    Of the young and old
Put to question your self practice
    Cease to do it for a time
It is not a question of in or out
    Rather, entrance through
    By way of sword or key

                              Corvallis, OR 10.27.03

*

Choose the fires to extinguish
We may have not sparked this one
    But we have neglected
"You mean this metaphorically?"
No
It is real
"Physically extinguish?"
Not always
It is not physical
    At most times
This urgency is much appreciated
    Yet undervalued
The world is wondrous
    When considered with divine implication

                            Covington, LA 2004

*

The bones of the young
    So pristine
Broken through trials
When aligned
    And healed
The fusion is stronger than inception

                  Corvallis, OR 09.23.03

*

Dead on arrival
Playing devil's advocate
    With a proud shield and cynical sword
Add confusion to the understood
    Façade of self confusion
Play the harp, so gentle, demon

                          Corvallis, OR 09.23.03

*

Woe to thee
Who revel-
    The violation
And weep
    With the punishment
There may be two
    Similarly afflicted
But blessed be the ashamed one
    For righteousness still dwells within you

                        Corvallis, OR 09.30.03

*

Wrought tears
    Did this
    Tempest of the mind
The reign
The reign
Flood my mind
Drown my ability
Fantasize about not needing
    The keys
Neglect
    There would be not a lock
Two paths
    One of push
    One of letting go
Ponder where you would
    Be headed
Fact remain
    Your death at stake

                    New Orleans, LA 09.26.2004

*

Truth is right
Yet strive not to be right
    But in truth
Argue aspects of truth
    As you understand
    But listen
All good teachers are students
Humbly, you could be wrong
In humility, you are right

                          Corvallis 04.12.03

*

Progressive thought
    And accountability to self
This is how a master is born
A master passes on lesson
    To those open to learning
"Is not that cheating them
    Out of their own experience?"
No
That is how a student
    Raises to heights above their own master
This is how a master is made

                  Portland, OR 01.13.09

*

Is not the intelligence
    Of the world
So dependent upon
    The intelligence
    Of the processor?
I had a near life experience
    I want you to come with me
What extraordinary phenomena
    So present outside
Is threefold within you
Something to pursue
    Inside you, throughout life
How then can expectation lie
    In conceptualizing another
    Let alone the celestial?
Yet leave not alone the celestial
Leave not alone your sister and brother
Quiet contemplator
    Witness to the truth
The light may reflect
    Or shine through

*

A shadow
    Not darkness, but a remnant of light
I am Shadow Catcher
I know about the fifty pound halo
    Such duty from conscience
Referenced not so much serpentine waters
    As decision without witness

Puff prayer pipe
    Smoke offered incense
Serenity enter lungs, in your breath
Peace past your lips
    Evacuate plight and anxiety
Enter a poverty, emptied
    Hungry for justice
Claim sanctuary
    From your
    Heart's war
The spectrum of humanity
    Ranges us
    From utmost wretched
To redemptive glorious
    Most beautiful
Angels envy us
    Though sin not of Cherubim
Sing so
    Seraphim
I beseech your aid in my endeavor
    To be human

*

Under the wreckage
    Of a human storm
Low day of reckoning ensues
Cursed for cursing
    My Freudian tongue
I have traveled, asunder
    Darkly regarded
For good reason
    In good judgment
For I played foolish
        Confused mercy in my life
        For reward

                                    Corvallis 2003

*

My shadow takes a stance
        As the sun is behind me
Save myself as you avalanche
        Down the mountain
But if you reach for me
        As will I go
I will let my limbs tell me
        How far
We are all refugees
        In need of our homeland
You cannot tell me
        The bird will not fly another way
Offer seed
        And watch attention pay
It is late
        For the ones without rest
I forgive
        But I cannot forget
A lion lurks in the heather
Let loose your heart
        Mind rational defense
Redirect to your soul
        And on sole you recover the bounty

                              Fairfield, CA 12.31.1993

*

Curse not your enemies
    If you are good
    As you believe to be
Bless your enemies
    They will curse themselves
We are weary of our own fault
In modernity we put our sin
    On the necks of the innocent
Through our derision
    We access the escape
Forty follies
    Lain upon
    Slain in public
Avoid these faults
    In tremor times

"The past is gone"
Is it now?
Your chronic disease revisits
    Your memory haunts
    Of past abuse
We wrestle masked foes with ominous names
A career ensues
    With broken bones and pins
Clear revelation of such pursuits
    A blessing to end
    As a schizophrenic masquerade

*

Ever yet the obedient student
        Impatience resides
Wearily I mock praised objects
        Teach me gold, paint, metal, wood, teach
Manipulated into forms
        The substance is constant and fulfills its purpose
        Like a soulful slave, making tyrants of hands
I thieved what is gifted
Now to open my eyes
        From being a dependent ingrate
Impatience versus gratitude, I turn
Thankful for the lesson
        I search for the teacher
Certainly not the object
        Concurrent epic
Certainly not I, the receiver
I thank the author

The unconcerned
        Have been dis-concerned
Curious scientists we are born
        Pursuant past our undeveloped eye
For this night
        This wine, evident on my breath
        Has taken me to a place
Ironically focused, concerned with significance
A time appropriate
        To take off my spectacles to see
A time when guttural voices
        Become tuning forks
Outside myself
        Outside controlled manipulations
How eager our senses when
        Calmed
        Collected
        Silenced
        Without sedation
How attuned the ear then
        To identify the drop of a pin
How affirmed the hungry tongue
        To the grain of the earth
As I go about this earth
        A stumbling fool
In attempts to talk
        I mumble
In attempts to do
        I bumble- without hindrance
Anxiety abounds
        So then time passes quicker through me
Incongruent with the truth

*

The arsenic will be placed
    In a cool drink
    On a hot day of turmoil
Mistake not summer as
    The sole season of embrace
Autumn softens a parched heart
And spring flowers flow
    From winter snow
The beginning of the year
    Is the birth
Born at the end
    I build from what we have
    Come to know
My fruit is then of autumn
    When often spring for others
    Lest it be my fall
    Because that is my time
I have once felt you
    Reopen my eyes to your splendor
I have not a stance
    Opposed to sitting
Nor do I sit on a stance
Harvest, celebrate, sleep
    In due time

*

All desire love and uniqueness
        To be special
Selfishness disguised as self efficacy
        Disquieted by injustice
Your trip is your own
        A lover moment to moment
Oh, Statue of Liberty can you
        Reach above those capitalizing
        On the vulnerable
        And on those socializing
        To take fortitude from the people?
Speak not a word ill-tempered
        Permissive upon debauchery's dismissal
Hot air of humanity sinks
        Deep into stale psyches
Strip away fear
        Peal away soft comfort
        And what you have is your core
Above water
        Above ground
        Above Ellis
Reach high, her light

*

We are so prone
    To take
And yet if we take
    The time
We would see
    That so much is out there
More than we
    Can receive

*

Able to recognize good will
    Racism
    Prejudice
    Discrimination
Sift, don't sour
I have been down
    These streets
    They shouldn't profile doubt
Stuck on the stoop
    Stay where their momma say
They rhyme
    With the same words
    They rhyme
It is so unbecoming
    Soon they become
    Contempt

Regurgitate pulse of others
    They- beaucoup trife
Katrina take your boy out of Nola
    No taking Nola out your boy
I haven't been rigged with rage
    My war drum
    Did not reverberate
Discovered their vertebrae
    Had no nerve
    Their spine no muscle
Recognize difficult challenge
    Not to roll with majority tide
    Not to polarize in minority pride
Contra flow
Able to recognize good will
    Peace of strength

Leave it to man
        To meander
        So aimlessly
To lose all purpose
        Wrapped up in pleasures
Animals fall prey
        When stagnant
Then must we ask
        What is our predator?

*

Desirous to be past
    Our struggles
And having obtained fortune
Let us be present minded
Fight for peace
    Call for silence
Live each day as it is your first
    Without desperate scramble
For we are on both sides
    Of fortune and struggle

*

Duty of conviction:
Measure the accountability
And deliver access
    To the masses

*

The "Oh" looks like "Eee"
    And the "Eee" then like "El"
Assuredly, your hole looks like Hell
Lo, Leo up high
Lift your eyes
    And your recovery nigh
Some things are wrong for some
    But not for others
Some things are wrong for all
Some things are all-right
    But other things right for none
It is not your right to decipher
    But you're obligation
Step forth with this designation

*

Simmer…
    Simmer
Glitter, glide
A fish of a new tide
Play and piddle
    You're going to get burned
Stutter, sputter
Dimmer…
    Die

                      Fairfield, CA 05.08.94

*

Oft plots granted to
    A fictional government
    To the persuasive storyteller
Feign disdain of tyranny
    Though oppose deposing tyrants
And what are these useful words
    Without service paid
    By scholars put to use
May my reputation be incurred
    As those favored words
    In so many eulogy
One must bid
    To do anything
A ship is set upon water
    As well as its sail and sailor
Be on deck or course astray

One day upon a hundred
It was no suckling-hunger
    But my forgotten, stooping effort
Revealed, rare breed
    Becoming a lasting namesake
I bear in both hands
    A private bounty for you
At what we grab
    We cannot grasp
Take only what is needed
We tire and toil ourselves
    In small minded endeavors
Between our grounded dreams severs
Saved by our eclectic bid
    That caught the eye looking
To the dry mangrove
    Temple of Ta Prohm
To honor ancient roots
    In contemporary time
    A vain foundation
If to find fountain of youth
    Behold
    The purgative flaming fountain

*

Early on I discovered
    With anecdotal evidence
Truth more apparent
    In the witnessing of avoidance
    Than in approachment
The disparagement of food
    So I fed the little duck
    Of the big flock
Yes the dawn displayed
    All in front of me
Though my eyes out of focus
    Persevered to squint
The names came to me
    Purpose shot through me
Until the titles were told to me
For that previous moment
    I absorbed prior
    To permeating

*

I stumbled upon a stool
    In the dark
    That I placed there myself
I was angered
If for the stool placed
    Self centered retreat
If for the pain
    I succumb to self-pity
If for myself
    Stumble upon accountability

*

In their proliferation
        The most robust rat
        Is the quickest
The most robust dog
        Is alpha
The robust sheep
        Is favored
But the most robust snake
        Is a cannibal
Be not a consumer of self
Look inward
        Only to attune
        To the expanse of Truth
Break free of your breed

*

The eternal chases me
      Like a father chasing
      His gleeful child
Though now, I forgot the game
A hunting that haunts me now
      When I ceased play
Became weary with poor stamina
Let my thoughts be akin to the words
      Calm the trite hysteria
Disenchanted by drug induced Oracles
I will callous my hands
      In these brief moments
      For an opus
This house of quality
      Only by earned merit
A power which induces
      Not revelry
      But responsibility

*

Ethereal promises arise from doubt
    Evaporate from truth pursuant
Unconscious, we are persuaded
One can only fully accept
    What one understands

Be like the fire
    Consumed and consuming
Desolating that which is rubbish
    Death for new life
Be like the water
    Quench and flow
    And cooler than the
    Environments surrounding
Be like the wind
    Sower of seeds
Be like the rock
    Solid, stabilizing
Internal rhythm vibrate
All this within your being

*

All inhabitants
    Born of goodness
    Have slight faith
This element enough
    For us to quest for more
And in the end
    Faith is all we have
In killing another
    We accept death proliferating
    Bond exterminated
Likewise, if to embrace life
    Recognize own iniquities
    And pardon
Proceed with pardoning, good shepherd
    Around you life resounds
Be thankful for your meal
    Ushered by the hounds
And for all you hold dear
    Ability to protect
Beseech pardon for missteps
    And you step on holy ground

*

Be it darkness or bright
    Both render one without sight
When engaging outside our element
In seeking sight
    Overcome the differentials
The flow of smoke shows
    Where the wind goes
And at its tail
    You can trail the impetus burn
Olly olly, follow it back home
    Or folly, indicate
    Your enemy

*

Worship in the beat
    Of swollen temples
Contentious bellies churn
Stomping feet of acclaimed rebels
    Such governments never settle
We take in more energy than we expend
Repressions converted to depressions
    And our economies sour
Internal quarrel turns plural
    Ripe was the hour
Failed at invoking vocation
Buffalo hunt
        Would give what one needs
        And one keeps what one received
        Cannot seize without chase

*

Madness abounds
    Burning blazing
Caught within an hour of eternity
This vibrancy rising
    Recognized as content-breaking
Redefinition of you
    But I heard your glory songs bashing
Any condemnation of a group by any one
    A scourge on society
Scorch with desire
    Trail blazer
Economies of size
    Moral inflation led to moral bankruptcy

*

Got a postcard from Vedder
    Says he's at the Taj Mahal
You know, it's funny
    This world seems so small
Sent the postcard to Portland
    Where he did a show
Lost the postcard, now
    All I have is a
Paper memory

                        Portland, OR 06.08.09

*

Smoke- living receipt
Fire erupts from smoldering debris
    Where I discarded the ashes
I still made it out with my life
    So in the end, I end up ahead

*

When tempted to quit
    Remind yourself of what it means
"I have given more than any other"
"I can give no more"
"Nothing is worth this"
A good heart objects

That act of blessing
        Superior to I
That act of love
        Greater than I
How blessed
        For I'm able to bestow

*

Coach called
    He replaced the receiver

*

When discovering
    A lesson to share
Do not number them
    Lest you assign value
Priority kept
    According to
    Deficiency of student

*

Rights infringe upon
    Other rights
And every opinion
    Is oppressive
What is left is weighed

*

Perhaps God's greatest
    Weakness
Is us
We personify the wicked wicks
    In crooked candle sticks
Carry on, carry on
    Like some Bristol hum
We brim with confidence
    We- all on our second day
    Of school

*

Evil transforms
Use
      Into misuse

*

The sky is blue
> Because it looks down upon
> All of humanity

*

One may state someone
    Is a certain label
It may be accurate
    But it is never the conclusion
Pursuit of that feeling
    Is oft the problem

*

The line between my truth and lie
Is Heaven and I
That lie is the distance between
Heaven and I
Depart from estrangement, enter

*

There is a man here
    I figured I'd never see again
At the time
    He assured me
    I could never say never
I greet him now
    But his memory does not recall
    It will never recall me
I'll never see that man again

                                Corvallis, OR 06.25.07

*

There is much relief
    In exhaustion
    Toil has taken all
I refer not to the rest
    But the aspect of having
    No other momentary concern

                      Salem 03.01.08

*

In lessons in love
People often want a receipt
    Before buying in
      To trust self abandon
A receipt cannot be rendered
Lest the lesson
    Be for not

                        Cloverdale, OR 12.29.09

*

What is longer?
A transformative day
Or
A minute of ego-babble?

                              Vancouver, WA 01.10.10

*

Baptized by the cemetery
Shalom
Significant for the city
    Than in a small town
If not blood,
    What makes the namesake wake?
Identity is not
    In recognizing what one is not
It draws the lines that make your shape
The theory remains theory
    And minds stay myth
Yet all these things
    Are hope and faith and you
    Renewed

                          Salem 03.11.09

*

Much like the value of sand
    Of an hour glass
    Is in the purpose of each grain
Such are we
We are the shore
    Of something great

*

What distinction in race have we?
We all,
      Between the whites of our eyes
      And our black pupil
Containing the color spectrum

                                      Salem 03.11.09

*

Aid in diverting my eyes
    Before I cease to see debauchery
So that I do not fail
    To see it in practice
I shall rejoice my tribulations
For recognition not only
    In temperance
But in the death of all that dwells
    In my heart that should not
Be it that anything worth bearing on mind
    Is weightily leaning on my skull
I have no right to anger
Like a disgruntled child
    Who is in need of slumber
For my wakeful hours have soured

                      Salem 03.11.09

*

When a dark day of pain
    Is met with rain
You may notch it a sorrow, and
    Lament it's cold, dark outcome
Better to rejoice
    Fully live
    This moment
With the lifeblood of crops
    Cleansing stale urban facades
This is not invitation
    To turn frown to smile
The smile is present in deceit
    Present with assumption
    Before the disturbance of reality
Nervous smiles serve all
    In the face of strangers
Such things are frivolous
Freed from that
    Rejoice in the vast composition
There is that ultimate chance
    To turn without crop or cleansing
What is the opportunity for yourself
    And for those around you

*

We are all uncertain in experience
    And contemplation
It is the glimmer of perfection
    Of something supreme
That makes the faithful

*

Dark figures in the distance
To what do I attribute?
    The distance between us
    Obscured mindset
    Accounting what got us here
    To what is happening
    Perceptional affect
    Special effect
Fault my vision to the clouds, rain, both
If dark figures becoming forefront
Right in front
    Belated action dispatches me

*

People are looking
      To fix
      For a fix
To be part of the fix
      Own the city
Not by building count
But by the hearts of the people

*

What we need is a prudent purveyor
A fingerless wine
      Won't touch you
Useless in panic
Like a kettle
      Whistling before the heat
Do with distinction
Abandon the process

*

My weaknesses
    They overcome me
    They are stronger than me
My strengths
    Weaker than me
    Inflate me
If only to use the strength
    Overcome the conceit

*

"Know it by heart"
    Does not say much
How properly acquainted
    Are we
        To our own heart?

*

I read an acclaimed book
    About
    The greatest of journeys
And discovered
That it must be read again

                             Portland, OR 01.07.09

*

Somewhere before the
    Precipice of relativity
Understanding the limits of my scope
But discarding the scope
    Leaves one without measure
Challenging my personal
    Paradigm
Is the wellspring to
    Revelation

                            Portland, OR 05.03.09

*

One should take no heed
    From a quack doctor prognosis
Over preventative
Medicine
But if that quack
    Says duck
One should duck

                          Portland, OR 07.10.09

*

Allow myself joy in my labor
    So it gives birth to life
In which I toiled and suffered
That I may be present
    In the suffering
Grateful for before the labor
    My troubles were greater
May I be delivered upon that day
    Among those hours

                         Salem 07.19.09 @0103

*

This world without me
>A darker place
>For a time

Change is always in order
If not your thought
>Change is in that order
>Will I be
>In the hearts of mankind
>Perhaps on the lips

Relevant enough to travel
>From evoked hearts

Provoking eager lips?

*

We chased the titles
    And subjects
All the while
The importance was
    Much more delicate
To you I dedicate
    The predicate

*

Looking up
    To atmosphere
There, in my sky,
    You are, starlet
Where is my representation?
Right near
There, the counterbalance

*

Throwing pearls
    To swine
Putting stock
    In iniquities
Not in giving someone in
    A poverty
    A chance
Poised when depleted

*

Taught in a glass-room
For immediate influence
Contribute to the
      Current trajectory
Young minds, rife ability

*

In significance
By population
In time
We are but one drop
    In the ocean
If we do not join
    We are a difference of two drops
    Becoming part of the restrictive forces
Consider our influence
    We are ten drops
Ripple effect
Consider the influences
    Passed to those we have affected
We are a tributary

*

Throughout this life
    Home comings abound
Building up, up, up through life
    But come trouble
        Evacuate through the bottom floor
But through no prodigal self assurance
    Serves me now
I have come home to die
    Outside resources offer nothing now
Pets wander away to pass
    Now I wander in
Oh how long have I been out
Returning now with tattered bounties

*

To appoint
    It takes an insider
To anoint
    It takes an outsider

*

Delusional
    And other ways
    To paint your sky
Are we just as the waves
    Crashing down on ourselves?
The most treacherous waters
    Come from what one conducts
Streaming from eyes
    Projecting deficiencies
Loss of sight

*

Economic seer
    One who
Keeps all
    Accountable

*

    One's body grows
        But in the process
    Diverging between
        Head and feet
    Furthering the gap
        Between concept and consummation

*

Pausing to recognize this burning ember
    My hand floats smoke
Ghosts that connect the present of
    What is
To the past of
    What was
To disassemble the structures
    Among the ancient trees
    To be placed in the forest
Up top a crow's nest
    Swishing branches in the night winds
    Reminiscent of perpetual tides
These hands grasp clubs, and arrows,
    And bows, and pipes, pencils,
    And fortification
Both what we fight with
    And what we fight for
To step outside one's self
    Then to convey the sacred
Hierarchy is necessary to facilitate
No place between artist, muse, and art
    Not between sides of a battlefield.

                        Portland, OR 02.23.09

All ideas are oppressive
    Defending against the contrary

Dispel your beliefs
    Witness small semblances
Small gradients point vastly
Beauty is the beginning
The start of every relationship
It draws us
    So we draw it
Be not afraid of advancing discovery
    Mystery is unobtainable

*

Is it not
    So possible to contrive
A conjecture so irrelevant
That it provokes discussion and
    Is provocative

*

It is not enough to be human
    "It is my nature"
Not a call to be superhuman
    Calling to be supernatural
To rise to the occasion
    Rise above
One must prepare in ordinary time
    In lieu of that occasion
If reserved to go by whim and whistle
It will get darker
    Than any night underground
Just because Auschwitz snow is not cold
    Should not comfort you

*

Defend the defenseless
Save the senseless
    Afford them at least
One more moment
    To come to realize
Each moment antiquates the next
Now you are acting out
    What you have scripted long ago
    Back then, seemed so apropos
Comfortable taking stations
    In times of war and depression
Do not know where you stand
    With your own turmoil
Once the noise drops

*

Frightful creatures feel the most fear
    Intoxicants are inept oracles
Nightmare recalled a memory
    Insincerely seeking seers
It's a bella sera
It's a bella vie
Crossed the konditorei
    Sip a spell on some coffee
Hitched a ride upon a troika
    Perception, preparation
    Poise
    Faith in hopeful love
Landed on a syzygy

*

We are a world of wars
    The wars begin from within
Muted voices to implore
    We are to blame for our myopic view
In time of distress
    Baby looks for one
    The mother of all inventors
When did the worship
    Cease to be holy?
When did the mystery
    Lose its mystique?
In the vast immensity
    Celebrating more unknown than known

*

For those who need
Syllables' inundation
      To grant attention
I'll leave you
To the prose

I

Being with you
> Milk and honey rhapsody

Demystify infatuation with you
Then enters love
And by you
> I am mystified again

Mature as art
> Like fine wine

Without love,
> We:
> > Aged vinegar

Flavors arise regardless
> Via time

Disrupt the onslaught of self destruction
> And choose, daily, to grow young together

We grow and welcome this third entity
> This love
> Binding us

How about that endeavor
> To decipher the language
> To study the art, to

Become the connoisseur
Squander one's self when
> Giving to the emergent

II

Emergent tremors betray
> Leading to quakes that decimate

Is not what you seek in the 2nd
> What you sought in the 1st?

Parting from this life together
> Without you
> Then my being would be departed

Your softest safest spot invaded
> Into your heart

The endeavor devoured me,
> Consuming my all
> Assimilating into your all

For true love is between two
> To split is to divide that love

*

    Unrequited delusion
    I have been deconstructed
        Now redefined
    You gave me heart
        I was intoxicated with purpose
    Now not detecting much flavor,
        Merely maintaining in this era of neglect
    Am I my own single admirer, nurturing my wounds
    No consultation to the third entity
My question turns me rhetorical
        Answering self, soliloquy
        "Seek another?"

III

    I hold you as you weep
        With your sorrow
    Your tears roll down my cheek
    Your tears become my tears
        The opposite of love
        Is the guise of love
    What is the purpose of the wayward glance?
        A quick read, for what information?
        Instinct over intent
        Something other than you
        Driving you
    Body facing me
        Face turned aside
    Effort doubtless partner- appreciation, love, and care
    You may like flowers, but have mercy
        Your starving garden
    You December like frost
        End this wicked season
    The flowers produced
    From that entity created between us
    The communication, the connection spills
        Confusion sets
    Why can she no longer see?
        Show her sight again

IV

    On hypocritical loins
        One leaps to another anybody
    All the while expending that effort
        That investment squandered
    Can never have that dirty laundry laundered

*

Every action leaves an indelible mark
> Be it pure or stain

Must we reconvene in our minds and remind our eyes?

Expose its farce:
> "Once lost, forever lost"
>
> Not to reconvene, but to convene again and

again
> Anew and always anew
>
> In those first days, when mystery marked

our ways

Unfamiliar to one another's days

And so there was that union

That crept in our hearts

Out of our eager eyes

Slept in our bellies

Life is hard, love softens
> Love hardens when mismanaged
> Through self preservation

I connect with her eyes
> Then I approach the rest of her being

We take this recognition of each other and cradle it

Considering the great struggle

Coming home from battle

So comforting to return to the sole duty of rest

At home to the arms
> Invited by the heart

Binding self to obligation frees me

I am fidelity
> I have faith in us

Every pearl has its price
> What ransom more worth while?

V

Physical love is accounted through acquisition
Amalgamation accounts for the spiritual
So to love in this world
> We acquire through coming together
> Both giving of self

As love has restored us as nebula stars,
Our obligation-
> To restore the light when it wanes

Restorative, ever new
> Awake in this
> Glorious morning

Patiently your passion grows

*

      Energized into the art
      And it draws your love closer
More than glittery and glistening, she is luminous
There is a physical manifestation of our third entity
      Our love, our life
Replete, let our brackish spirits rise
Through our time together
      Your name changes with me
      First "enigma, desire"
      Eventually "destiny"
      And through so many more "Lover"
All these and more
By the day
This final chapter
      Is the first of ours
In the break of every day
Turn toward your touch
      Sprinkle petals without thought much
The rapturous fortune
Let us be the everlasting cadre of love
I pledge all this forever and
      Ever Afterglow

*

◊ ◘ ◊ ◘ ◊   OUTRODUCTION   ◊ ◘ ◊ ◘ ◊
CANTUS

Why "Cantus"? Cantus, the word, in Latin means "song", a reference to the poetic affiliation of Canto… This is my own song, and hopefully it belongs in the hearts of humankind. The title was written in the supposed "dead language" of Latin- that is deceptively very much alive and influential in modern languages. It was once a universal language and continues to permeate our communication today. I use Latin in naming my premier book, akin to science in naming species in the interest to use a global language in identification. These elements of life are out there for our perceiving which then leads to a higher meaning. These words are not a directive to take a stance, rather to take to a movement.

Why Cantus? The reason for writing this book has much to do with my inclination since age 13 to write poetry. The words came first, then very shortly after- the meaning. Then the importance set in. Now, I feel the imperative to share it with anyone who will be able to stop in their busy daily life and enter into something deeper. What importance am I to my community or generation or the aeons of those preceding or following? Good question. I do not know. But I can say this is important and I believe it enriches all who contemplate its depths.

These poems are meditations as well as songs. I sing them and at once I both treasure them for their elemental human rhythms and release them to an audience. This book is a reflection. There is a greater reality than what any one person can capture, but this text is an introduction into the greater part of our lives than we often neglect. It is a step forward in that pursuit. When you read "I" or "You" in the text, consider yourself on both sides. Ultimately an indictment to one is a call for accountability to all. Surely, I do not presume to be greater than my own perspective, yet I feel a gift to formulate these words and an imperative to introduce this to you and simultaneously responsibility for myself.

My style is concise and direct, my words are strictly intentional- so you will not be panning for what I think is gold. I will offer to you my thought and you can trust that there is much to be examined in that text. I may from time to time offer a short journey, but that too is to serve a strict purpose- to arrive to an idea.

So in the deliberation over what here I write… take it in slowly. You be the judge once you consider this: process but a few poems in one reading. Unless you feel a connectedness that flows, that permeating contemplation- then, by all means, continue on. I offer my email troika7@gmail.com for questions and discussion.

Curiosity holds the beauty of discovery and positions one for learning which is more fruitful than those who have preconceived notions. I list titles which were named in reference to a specific line or phrase in the poem, as to not impose an idea. Listen. Cantus.

:::center
*

𝔇𝔬𝔰𝔢

Poems of Quintessential Ethereality

Brad Dehler

TROIKA STUDIOS & PUBLISHNG
SALEM, OREGON
:::

*

Dose: Poems of Quintessential Ethereality

Copyright © Brad Dehler 2016, 2025

ALL RIGHTS RESERVED. No part of this work covered by the copyright herein may be reproduced, transmitted, stored, or used in any form or by any means graphic, electronic, or mechanical, including but not limited to photocopying, recording, scanning, digitizing, taping, Web distribution, information networks, or information storage and retrieval systems, except as permitted under Section 107 or 108 of the 1976 United States Copyright Act, without the prior written permission of the author.

Printed in the United States of America
3rd Edition

Additional copies are available at
https://www.createspace.com/3514742
or www.Amazon.com

For product information, permission to use material from this text, or further permissions questions- please e-mail to: Troika7@gmail.com

---

Book design and layout: Brad Dehler
Both photographs: painting by and portrait of the author

ISBN-13: 978-1-966716-01-3
ISBN-10: 1-966716-01-X

Troika Studios & Publishng; Salem, Oregon
Printing by CreateSpace & KDP; Charlotte, South Carolina
An Amazon Company
USA

Other Troika Publishng books by Brad Dehler:
Cantus: A Book of Poems
(ISBN-13: 978-0-982-97330-1 & ISBN-10: 0-982-97330-6)
https://www.createspace.com/3481170
http://www.amazon.com/Cantus-Brad-Dehler/dp/0982973306/

Brad Dehler's "Cantus" is a litany of meditations that are contextualized by the immense space that can magnify meaning: small phrasings, by design, appear larger on the physical page. This is not incidental. It is the poet's economical task of saying more with less.

Here is a collection that is as philosophical as it is poetic, channeling the existential being-in-thought that breathes life into those unafraid of not knowing. The exhale between "songs" affirms: getting lost in its music is imperfectly okay.

- **Tim'm T. West**, Poet, educator, and author of "Red Dirt Revival", "Flirting", and the latest "pre|dispositions"
TruAtRedDirt@gmail.com

DOSE
Table of Contents

Bring Forth The Light	12
Golden Heart	13
All The Blended Fruits	14
Bends Your Knee	15
Future Is Illusion	16
Broken Hopes On Slippery Slopes	17
Rich	18
Troika	19
Sweet Sweat	20
Occupied Territory	21
Take A Trip	22
Night Time Revival	23
Climb Up The Mountain	24
Things I Imagined	25
Beware Inertia	26
Walks Alone	27
Mythic Beast	28
I'll Always Love You Again	29
Martial Law	30
Attache Attached	31
New Refugee	32
Questions	33
The Exhaulted	34
Enemy Of Truth	35
Frontiers Yet Still	36
All Now	37

*

Float Vulnerable	38
Second's Satisfaction	39
Our Land In Jeopardy	40
Come Back Now	41
Last Assessment	42
Life Through Liver	43
Energy Will Not Cure	44
Get Lake	45
Discovered Me, Asleep	46
All This Pain	47
Come Back Down	48
Misplaced Bemoanings	49
Do Not Burn Them	50
Privileged Misfits	51
Latent Entities	52
Red Heron	53
Ask Yankton Ask Nakota	54
Of The Fall	55
Impending Room	56
Small Screens	57
Surf-ride Tides	58
I Write In Exile	59
Without Arrows	60
Truly Fulfilled	61
This Is A Recovery	62
Alumni	63
Two Options	64
Your Feet Will Find	65

Demons In White	66
Descend The Stairs	67
Knocking Against My Will	68
Our Alms Out	69
Passion Finances	70
Dulcet Dreams	71
Truly Love Me	72
Once One Knows	73
To Touch Paper Then Beyond	74
No Time	75
Talk About The Revolution	76
Treat With Cream & Sugar	77
Supported The Faction	78
Dependent Upon The Hungry	79
Why To Believe	80
In A State Of NOLA	81
Unsound Jury	82
A Good Thing	83
Sacrafice Is Sacred	84
To Take You Down	85
Much Like Love	86
The Deep Look Inside	87
Harrassing A Hawk	88
After I Awoke	89
Of An Idol	90
Bulleted Texts	91
Why Did It Mean So Much	92
Dossier To Destroy	93

Ill Niche	94
Drive Made Real	95
Adopt A Highway	96
More Without You	97
All Bridges Most Valuable	98
I Know Paradigm	99
Dim Witty	100
Coming Home	101
I Found Myself	102
Delivered	103
Let Me Be That For You	104
Until Put To Pavement	105
Calibrate With The Know	106
We Are Both	107
Moral/Morale	108
Great Plains	109
Atrocious Notions	110
Scars That Split	111
There Was A Ghost	112
You Develop Venom	113
Break Some Bread	114
I Want You To Have	115
For The Exalted	116
I Have Been Broken Down	117
Living On A Dead End	118
Small Enough To Care	119
Making Our Love	120
Wage Preservation	121

Maiden Landscape	122
Slow Birth	123
Hypoxic Parachuters	124
A Line Can Be Drawn	125
Have A Great Day	126
No Merit	127
Bard's Anagram	128
Strike-Strike	129
The Drum Inside Us	130
Soil Epiphanic	131
Power Of The Lesson	132
I Wont To Go	133
	134
	135
	136
	137
	138
	139
	140
	141
	142
	143
	144

INTRODUCTION
DOSE

Thank you for choosing Dose. This is my sophomore book, succeeding my first book "Cantus". I chose the title "Dose" for various reasons. First off, I want to minimize the preconceptions that follow labeling, minimal in one word. Another reason is that I hope that these words, stanzas, poems are healing and supportive of life- as a dose of true medicine. Finally, the title phonetically resembles the word "dos" which means "two" in Spanish.

Why Cantus? Why can't we? Why Dose? Why don't we? Where Cantus was me, stepping out in "singing", my vocation out loud; Dose is a second offering that again collects poems from the past and present -to be read in the future with a focus on internal change. We are in this life together for the time being. The questions and conclusions posited here are a call to action for which all are accountable. These imperatives absolutely include me. I have not perfected what I propose within the text, I attempt to display it as it is revealed to me.

These poems are medicine as well as a challenge. It can be bitter and unpleasant, confounding and triumphant. The only way it works, though, is by internalizing. I hope that you find these poems relevant to your life- and with that, integrated in a universal human experience.

*

I composed these poems in various States and various phases of my life. I began writing at age thirteen and instantly knew that there was a message to record and that the message was greater than I am. Take each poem slowly, removed from the regular toil of daily life. Enter a reflective and meditative state. Then perhaps what I offer here can take it further.

The title of each poem is based on a specific line of that particular poem. I do this to reduce convoluting the message.

The formula is organic; I attempt to remove over thinking and meddling with words- to avoid superseding the message, to place the words close to how they arrive initially in mind. I have learned to reduce contrived manipulation. This is where I believe the heart and head converge fairly equitably.

Now step out, lay back and remove yourself from the day-to-day. Take the Dose.

*

Do not tremble in the dark
For that which lurks
   In the dark
Trembles in the light
Bring forth the light

                New Orleans 07.06.05

*

Golden heart be attentive
Rubber souls get walked on
A faultless vase
    Resonates with a knock
The audience
    Does not have it all
    On the line
So decision should be made
    From within

Salem 01.09.11

All the blended fruits
    Of the merriment
All the twisted troops
    Of the regiment
All the moments that
    Make the momentum
What is the path?
    A mazy glade?
    A suspended balance beam?
Something in your efforts
    And once passed up
It is missing
    It is missed
Set out on
    The Hallowed venture
To end remiss

                Salem 03.23.08

*

Something so magnificent
    By its presence
    Bends your knee
Loss of dominance
    In your element

                      Corvallis 2000

*

Future is illusion
Past is delusion
All we have is
    Now

                    Salem 08.31.10

*

Broken hopes on slippery slopes
Hope into the void
    When devoid of hope
Ridiculous to believe in it
    While in acquisition
Though destined are the
    Fruits of fruition
The struggle can produce
    Self-fulfilled prophesy
Awareness is fundamental
We are poor prophets
    And sightless psychics
Hopeless in our misfortunes
Kindle that peat moss
    For future torch

                      Portland 10.18.15

*

Bless me
So that I can bless you
Bless you
So that you can bless others
We are all now keen
Our lives richer

                                        Salem 03.17.13

There is a troika
    Heading in a direction
In attempts to salvage
The perishable
We are apathetic or preoccupied
We are not responsible
Until
What is in us is entropic
    Or sinister occupation
The third horse, most powerful
    Able for change in direction
    Is the choice
The glorious change is
    Salvation of permanence

Salem 2007

*

When time is right
There is nothing sweeter
Than salty sweat

                        Salem 10.23.13

*

You are occupied territory
Not to be preoccupied
   With recognition
Aim to remain re-occupied
Possessed by the spirit

                  Modoc Forest, CA 06.23.16

*

Take a trip
Everywhere I go,
    I take my life there
Those actions ascribed
    To those every moments
Take a hiatus
    Anywhere
Right here
Had a sensation though
Could not determine which
    Sense told me so
Take out of here
Give it to what
    Was stifled inside

                Salem 08.09.10

*

Introspective
Make for change
Night time revival

                Utah 1998

*

A child looks up to adults
As a great mystery
    Full of understanding
The assumption is that age
Takes the climb up the mountain
The truth is that most
    Wallow down at basecamp

        New Orleans 2005

*

The things I imagined
Are really not as great
But those things in the expanse
Far exceeding my imagination

                Salem 2009

Beware inertia
Bodies at rest
Motion against resistance
    Imbibing to gravity
Anger perpetuates
The waves surge into us
    I am charged
Stand up, gear up
    I leave armed

                Salem 04.21.11

*

There is a chorus from
    The meadows
Time has come to stop and
    Inhale deep
Steam rising from your brow
Stopped to make camp
    That was then
    The tremor time
A prost to your good work
    This far, thus far

See now
    New and lavish arising
The Kinnikinnick travels with
Goodbye familiar friend
    Hello new curious friend
The winds started as a whisper
    Something light
Just enough to lift a feather
The wind escalating
Send some Kinnikinnick down
The earth is quaking underfoot
In the advent of immanence
    Imminently in the air
Revelatory nature
This woman
    Walks alone in the crowd
    She makes sound
    Within the noise

                      Albany, OR 06.2011

*

Do you understand
That I am just a man
My actions can be superhuman
    Reach past my will
My ideas are super-hue
… Would lead to love eventually
The mythic beast of
    Desire quenched
Came alive

                              Salem 04.18.11

*

I thought it impossible
    To satiate this voracious
    Appetite
Have these passing years
    Lulled the dragon to sleep?
I was once like a goldfish
    With propensity to binge
    All the way to death
Believing that the latest bite
    May be the last
Bite as hindsight
    Revealed the mere filler

Our love contains nutrients
    Truly resolving hunger
Alas I hunger again,
Alas I'll always love you again

                    Salem 04.30.08

*

Do not worry
I have a gun
They declared martial law
Times like these
    Taking to head counting
Others taking headshots
The sum
    Is not the person

                    New Orleans 07.20.06

*

Attaché attached to desolation
The wounded still-twitch
Baggage sighted oblivion
All in need
Do not tend to your deficiencies
This world is poor
    When we cannot put
    Our deficiencies aside
Curves seduce
The paved way slides from underfoot

                            Salem 12.08.10

*

I was prepared to evacuate my house
I was not ready to evacuate my city
It was a season of migration
New refugee
Legends without recorded histories
A walk amongst kings
    Few and far between
Closest thing to divinity
    Engendered in nature
It was the forest
    That invited the silence
And it was the silence
    That invited the quiet

                      Flower Mound, TX 10.2005

*

Feel not threatened
   By the questions
The questions exist
   Without their posing

                  Salem 02.11.11

*

For the exalted,
There must be one
    Taking number
    Away from the glory

                    Salem 11.18.10

Enigmatizing
What is plain in front of you
Serving the purpose
    Of serving yourself
Abandoning the duty
    Of bridging the gap
Between right and wrong
So
When the contrary
Is evidenced forth
You have sided
As enemy of truth

                      Portland, OR 01.22.10

*

Unconscious hours
Are swept, slept through
There are frontiers yet still
Doubt tells you it's been covered
But new eyes
    Open new worlds

                   Salem 06.03.11

*

Future is illusion
    Past is delusion
All we have is now

                Salem 08.31.10

*

Clouds do not float
    They are falling
I grew and stumbled
    Upon rocks
I was challenged
    By great fields
And intimidated by the forest
Water; life-source
I was summoned
    As we all are
To the ocean
It is and I loved
The tide rolled and
I float vulnerable

        Salem 04.17.06

*

Those in avid belief
    That lessons are only learned
    Through experience
Close their ears to sirens
For a second's satisfaction

                        Corvallis, OR 05.09.1999

*

You asked our age
    And assumed limits
We told you
But we did not ask of yours

That would be rude

You asked to share land
We opened our arms
    Knowing it is a part
    Of all of us
You poisoned yourself
    Burned, scorched, and sold
Our land in jeopardy

                    Portland, OR 02.14.11

*

Always thinking throughways
Could not predict sunken sideways
All those messages
    That do not have voices
All those worthy voices
    I did not receive
Come back down
    I see now folly

                      Salem 06.04.11

*

Anatomy of a car crash
When distracted
Attention switches to
    Arising situation
The argument
The spilled water
Most urgent because most emergent
Eyes abandon the road
Last assessment of road
    Copacetic

                      Salem 10.23.13

*

It is not
Always head versus heart
What about
    Life through liver

				Salem 03.25.13

*

```
    No external remedy to distraught
Like a happy pill
    For depression
Energy will not cure
    My exhaustion
```

                    New Orleans 07.06.05

*

River of deceit
Dam it
Make lake of fire

                Salem 03.20.14

*

There was a troubling sound
That resounded like a voice
Something that gave voice
    To despair
Rousing me from slumber
Seeking signs in imagined shadows
Do another parameter check
No founded proof
Resorting to prayer
In hopes to reach outside my power
Undoubtedly, the demon
    Peered in the open window
And in many hapless acts
    Discovered me, asleep

                      Salem 07.04.11

*

Administering the shock
    Because we were told so
We accept
We have witnessed
That is how
    We are apathetic
To all this pain

                        Portland, OR 10.25.15

*

Once you reach your dreams
Won't you come back down?
May the joy of contentment
Be yours

                            Salem 08.22.11

*

Songs of freedom
Cries of peace
Arriving in concert
To listen to what you
    Want to hear
Misplaced bemoanings
Dad abandoned
    And
Mom did not know how to love
They were lost at sea
    Overwhelmed
You are lost at sea
    Inundated
Drowning
Howling

                    Salem 10.12.15

*

I turn the chapters
Cross the bridges
Nay, I do not burn them

                        New Orleans 07.09.05

*

Privileged misfits fall
   Within their tier
There is a cheap and fast
satisfaction
   With candy and with anger
A whole other satisfaction
   With bread and butter
Laborers are left behind
After project culmination
Fatigue on the face
   Can look like wisdom
   The apparent knowing smile
Decoding labyrinths
   Glory only within that architect

                Salem 08.30.11

*

```
Inside your contentment
    Are
Latent entities
Known only through serenity
Disturbed,
    They will coup
```

                    Portland, OR 11.22.10

*

Red heron had been plucked
Feather by feather
No capabilities of flight
Pale placid skin exposed
Yet can be given flight
    By mere man's conjecture

                Salem 03.04.13

*

Ask Yankton
Ask Nakota
Knock lights out
Call it supernova
Tell the new guard
We have been here before
    All along
The vegetation and waterways
    That divide
Yield those who swim and step
Ask those who have trekked
    Climbed, crawled
Good counsel

                          Salem 11.18.10

*

Divinity speaks to our souls
We deviate from ourselves
　　To not hear our souls
That feeling that won't leave
Of the fall, loss of all

　　　　　　　　Corvallis, OR 09.18.01

*

This impending room
Fill it with sights and sounds
My incredulous eyes widen
   As they did
When I scant see nothing at all
Content is not satisfied

                    Salem 08.09.10

*

Do not focus
Too much on the small screens
In the big picture

                        Corvallis, OR 10.12.1998

*

Retreat from obligation
Surf-ride tides
Disheveled appearance acceptable
I would call it
My days in the sun

                        Salem 09.01.11

*

That radiating core
Native roots
    Tangled together
    In my carriage
I write in exile
I sing of release

                      Salem 08.31.10

*

An aim that revealed the target
But missed
Such is the world
Without the understanding
Without arrows

        Portland, OR 01.03.11

*

I felt so alive
I had consumed enough
Not truly fulfilled unless
I had truly hungered

                        Salem 06.22.11

*

Negotiating,
    Balancing dissatisfaction
Failing beget wagering over waging
Landslide begins
The collapsing landscape
    Clings to its dead
This is a recovery
    Not a rescue

                      Salem 03.28.14

*

When you are
Because you have been
Blessed alumni

                    Portland, OR 01.16.11

*

When you are that hungry
You have two options
Eat or go to work

                            Salem 07.10.11

*

As you regret shattered glass vase
Left to pick up the shards
What your hands do not grab
Guided by your eyes
Your feet will find

                          Salem 08.28.10

*

You hapless morose
You desperate lament
You simple sought accomplice
Internal politics leading
    To external threat
Nature to look
    For angel in black
Discover surplus
    Demons in white

                        Salem 07.08.13

*

For years
Earning the way up the floors
One day called to the top
To descend the stairs
Dismissed

                      Portland, OR 01.15.11

*

Knocking against my will
Open the door
To this glorious mourn
The sun shines on turmoil
Must not let it set
    On regret

                          Salem 07.22.10

*

Must we be broken
    Before fixing
Our alms out?

   Salem 09.04.10

Passion finances the war
    Between the beloved
Conversion to hurt until bankrupt
Will needed to re-collect affinity

                      Portland, OR 11.15.10

*

The pain is a venue
The struggle an avenue
Accessible among the trees
    Within you
I see myself reflected
    In your eyes
Struggles led you to a state
    That was beneath you
Out from your core
It was under your feet
    All along
Keep you grounded
Now you kneel, now you sit
    Now you lay
Dulcet dreams

                Salem 11.17.10

Regardless of any surveys
All I can account for
    Is that those
Who truly know me
Truly love me

                      Portland, OR 11.15.10

*

One can only know others
Once
One knows one's self

                        Salem 11.18.10

*

The spiritual, philosophical, political
Micro-mezzo-macro
In no particular order
The void pathologizes spirituality
Awareness gives literacy
Gives authority
The oblivious to incompetent
In a moment of zen
    I put it down to pen
To touch paper then beyond

                  Portland, OR 11.29.10

*

```
There is no time
    Except now
So now
    Is the time
```

                                        Salem 11.07.15

*

There is talk about the
    Revolution
Problem
    Rebels have no constitution

                    Portland, OR 11.29.10

*

Oppose our tendencies
Bitterness abounds, inevitable
   Treat with cream & sugar
Bill this world as a debt and credit
   Debt to justice
   Credit to love
To break tendencies
   It takes tending

                Vancouver, WA 01.2.11

*

I was privileged enough
To cover my eyes
    During the war
Right or wrong
I supported the faction
That would not enslave me

                      Pacific City, OR 07.05.11

*

I want a shot at the title
What to do when I get there?
Exhausted, depleted of resource
Yet the battle is not settled
The privileged are dependent
    Upon the hungry

                          Salem 10.28.10

*

I cannot tell you
    Why to believe in your dreams
Mine have yet to come true
But belief is the only way
    They will
Will they?
Will you?

                    Portland, OR 11.15.10

*

In a state of NOLA
What's more than
   A club in a car
Hatchet in the attic

              New Orleans 08.26.04

*

The trial should be in the mind
But you determined you knew me
    Prior, as a prejudice
So that the jury
    Was out of the sound
And the judge from out of the sight

              Salem 03.05.14

*

It is a good thing
For the most part
Uh oh
Stop me
Before I start

                        Corvallis, OR 11.15.1999

Any sacrifice is sacred
It is how we
Physically pray

      Portland, OR 07.10.11

*

What they will not admit
    Is they never thought much of you
Working your way up
All they want
    Is to take you down

                              Portland, OR 01.20.13

*

The new food is different
An experience
    More acquainted in youth
A curiosity that kept me searching
New and different
Much like love

                       Salem 07.31.11

Being aware of what
    They want you to think
Is the first line of defense
Against manipulation
Being aware of how
    They really feel
Is the first steps into insight
Yet beyond all this
    The deep look inside

                       Salem 10.31.13

You see those little birds
Harassing a hawk
After a distance
    Most peel away
Yet there is one little bird
    Snipping
The substantially larger hawk abides
Despite all ability
    To conquer the small challenge

                Cloverdale, OR 06.23.13

*

It was only after
    I awoke
That I realized
    I had fallen asleep
And then onset shame
Relent, repent
I have weathered
    Many such storms
This one is different
This one tethered

                  Salem 02.10.13

Hanging on every word
    Of an idol
Over issues
    Esoteric, intangible
Inconsequential insignificance
Idle
To my mind, my involved sage
Is to not complicate

            Portland, OR 02.23.14

*

Let me be a critic
    To the archetype
    As best of friends are
Neither opposer nor supporter
Impossible to separate
    Any persons
    From their paradigm
A thousand rifles
    Far too much
    For one man to handle
Yet
    Far too little
    To defend a nation
Yeah
    The man can recruit
    And nation convert
But consider the bullet that
    Ends the empire's emperor
Incendiary bulleted texts
    With similar aim
    I may offer
For war is too loud
    To hear this offering
And peace time
    May be cannabis to the masses

                Salem 07.2009

*

Asking why did it mean so much
Stubborn deadlock
Time expired to anguish
Squandered so much
    Did it mean
Why

                Corvallis, OR 09.30.1998

*

```
Little did I know
That the vitae
    I submitted
Was part of the dossier
    To destroy me
```

                Salem 02.01.14

*

Ill Nietzsche
Nihilism well played
Worshipped self
You are gone
Your god is dead

                        Portland, OR 02.07.08

*

Dreams are ideas
    Not of this world
For those not handed fortune
Only come to fruition
    With Drive made real
Be ridden of things that do not
    Drive you
Driven by the knowledge of
    All things that could rid you

                        Salem 01.03.11

*

Adopt a highway
Raise it as my own
Only one bathed in sun
Well-traveled
Attach my name
Complexities rising
Take it easy
Meet Keno in Reno

                    Reno, NV 06.24.16

*

You know more without you
Than within you
More of the moon
Than your ocean
The objective point of view
    Far more piercing

                      Salem 11.29.10

Being in untruth
    Your answers are questioned
Getting technical definitions
    Of depravity
    And corruption
Not a failure
    You failed again
Label akin to impossibility
No cycles, new day
Work from memory
    There's the lesson
Recognize
    Pattern the elements
    That cause virtue
Never "not yourself"
    Troubled times- new challenges
Open yourself to greatness
All bridges most valuable
    When the big ones burn

                    Corvallis, OR 2000

*

There is no reality
    Outside my own
    That of which I know
I know paradigm
Equating to two cents

                Salem 11.29.10

*

Your fictional mind
    In a non-fictional world
Quite the imagination
Dim witty
Dragon your fate around
Have mercy on your soul
That plays for keeps
Keeper for reals
I think I will stay
    I like the vibe tonight

                    Salem 01.08.16

*

This is no cycle for me
It is a one way track
Low hope to come back
Heading toward the storm
Losing my warmth
Reason why we do this
    Coming home
Operating in self
Serving shadows
Relying upon some dark horse

                        Portland, OR 10.07.10

*

Living the dream
Feeling life is unreal
Sensing it is surreal
I found myself
    In a situation
And in that situation
    I found myself

                 Salem 12.30.15

*

The way it is
    Delivered
Can bring
    Perspective

               Salem 02.18.16

*

Beacon of hope
Bastian of love
Purveyor of charity
The sword and salve of justice
Let me be that for you

            Salem 02.01.16

*

Evilness lives on silenced lips
Even a lie invites
    Dialog roots out truth
Power structure resists
    Change and evaluation
There is a continuum
    And it is finite
Theory is ideal
Until put to pavement
A king's portion
    A Cesarean section
The light on in the city
    Turns off the starlight

                      Salem 01.20.11

*

When it comes to pass
The lies
    Will lie down to truth
The confused
    Will kneel and bow and know
The insolent
    Will bow and break
You tamper with lies in illusion
    Of breaking paradigm
I reassure all who
    Have ear to listen
The urgency is to calibrate
    With the know

                Portland, OR 07.24.09

*

We are both
On this side of hell
And
This side of heaven

                    Salem 03.21.15

Neither above moral
Nor above morale

        Corvallis, OR 04.27.1999

*

Rumbling, rolling over the
Great Plains
Opposite the insignificant
No surprise
    The spoils were squandered
Ustoll the soil
Because our hopes are hung
On heroes and stars
Does not mean our hope
    Is suspended

                    Salem 01.22.11

*

Atrocious notions
    When we were kids
Are enacted in our adulthood
    As if licensed by age

                  Salem 01.09.11

*

The Scars that split
    Us in half
Before and after the event
Confusion
    Rendering us duplicitous

                Salem 03.20.16

*

There was a ghost
You breathed your warmth
Into the frozen
    Northern sky
Came back a cold front
Unrecognizable

                Portland, OR 01.03.11

*

You develop venom
Fangs to inflict
Yours is a kiss
   Of a serpent

              Salem 04.12.16

*

Do not be scared of open places
Everything is in its place
Settle down,
    Just have a seat
Break some bread
    It's more than 'eat'

                Salem 04.28.16

*

Something grips the heart
Kickstart
In hot pursuit
Corners rounding
Pounding into rhythm
Into an anthem
I got something
I want you to have

                      Portland, OR 01.03.11

*

For the exalted
There must be one taking number
Away from the glory

            Salem 11.18.10

*

Not lonely, but lone
Just as I am untrusting, but loan
Now I have been broken down

                Corvallis, OR 09.29.1999

*

Living on a dead end
Enter a river bend
Passing time
Skipping river stones
Educated in academia
    When paying intuition

           Vancouver, WA 12.24.10

*

Can you big enough to deliver?
Can you be small enough to care?

                              Salem 05.18.14

*

We go backwards
But we also go forwards
All the while
Getting closer
We did it together
Making our love

                Salem 05.03.16

*

Disregard waging war
    Or peace
Wage preservation
    Of universal value

                Portland, OR 07.24.09

*

```
I plucked the apple
    From the tree
    For you
I wrote the book
    On your skin
All those rain drops
They wash away
The lady in the
    Maiden landscape
```

                    Salem 07.27.16

*

Rest on the off season
Routine meal time
   Will remind you
At that absent minded moment
Pounds of pressure
Pounding out the measure
   Of a man
It is a slow birth
The dark night of the soul
Turned to years
Internal turn outward

                Portland, OR 11.22.10

*

Separated we take
Together we make
We are all but
Hypoxic parachuters

               Salem 10.26.16

*

Claim to a correlation
Leaving room to disclaim
A line can be drawn
    Between any two points

               Salem 02.28.14

*

Have a great day
Her words echo in my mind
    Not once, twice- thrice
As I left out in the world
Soon those words I thought
And the voice was my own
I will be under the rubble
    Some other
The day is made

                    Portland, OR 10.25.10

*

Goodness can proceed from evil
    But it does not beget
And all along the way
There is no merit
    In it
For you

                      Portland, OR 07.24.09

*

Bard's anagram
Will take me
Back home

                New Orleans 03.2005

*

Strike-strike, hit twice
    Before you roll the dice
I am in fight shape
Raining strikes
Until the foe has lost fight
Please, please
    Learn to never doubt on me
Down to one knee
We assimilated the same way

                  Salem 10.07.15

*

Beats give reference
    To past beats
The drum inside us
The last sonata
Those are the happy songs
In gloom
    The beats dissipate sharply

                Corvallis, OR 10.02.1998

*

Love is youthful
Yet
Youth can be frantic confusion
The soil of many trampled lands
Feel new in tender hands
With love, that soil epiphanic
    Sprouting seeds

                Salem 02.20.14

*

```
Human weakness
    We revere what
    We understand
Power of the lesson
    If we can appreciate
A 360 Degree view, but
From one position
```

                Salem 04.09.06

*

We climb
And climb and climb and climb
Some more
When at mountains' top
We discover
The oxygen poor air
The jagged cares
The frigid atmos fear
I wont to go

                        Salem 05.29.16

*

*

*

"(The) rhyme and images and musings... are intriguing. (Brad is) a deep thinker, thought provoking... on a quest to find meaning and treasures in life"

-**Millie Renfrow** Seattle Poetess; Co-author of "Between Light and Shade", recipient of the Phyllis Ennes award, and Associate of Seattle's "It's About Time Writing Series"

Cantus: A Book of Poems
Paperback ISBN-13: 978-0-982-9733-0-1 & ISBN-10: 0-982-97330-6
Hardcover ISBN: 978-0-982-9733-3-2
Paperback (5x8) ISBN-13: 978-1-966716-00-6 & ISBN-10: 1-966716-00-1
http://www.amazon.com/Cantus-Brad-Dehler/dp/0982973306/

Dose: Poems of Quintessential Ethereality
Paperback ISBN-13: 978-0-982-9733-1-8 & ISBN-10: 0-982-97331-4
Hardcover ISBN: 978-0-982-9733-4-9
Paperback (5x8) ISBN-13: 978-1-966716-01-3 & ISBN-10: 1-966716-01-X
https://www.amazon.com/Dose-Quintessential-Ethereality-Brad-Dehler/dp/0982973314

Syzygy: Poems of Essential Theory
Paperback ISBN-13: 978-0-982-9733-2-5 & ISBN-10: 0-982-97332-2
Hardcover ISBN: 978-0-982-9733-5-6
Paperback (5x8) ISBN-13: 978-1-966716-02-0 & ISBN-10: 1-966716-02-8
https://www.amazon.com/Syzygy-Essential-Theory-Brad-Dehler/dp/0982973322

Shadow Catching: Poems of Existential Peering
Paperback ISBN-13: 978-0-982-9733-6-3 & ISBN-10: 0-982-97336-5
Hardcover ISBN: 978-0-982-9733-7-0
Paperback (5x8) ISBN-13: 978-1-966716-03-7 & ISBN-10: 1-966716-03-6
https://www.amazon.com/Shadow-Catching-Poems-Existential-Peering-Brad-Dehler/dp/B0BMY5M9CN

Epiphaneia: Lost Poems of Epistemological Endeavor
Paperback (5x8) ISBN-13: 978-0-982-9733-8-7 & ISBN-10: 0-9829733-8-1
Hardcover ISBN: 978-0-982-9733-9-4
https://www.amazon.com/Epiphaneia-Lost-Poems-Epistemological-Endeavor/dp/0982973381

*

Poems of Essential Theory

Brad Dehler

TROIKA STUDIOS & PUBLISHNG
SALEM, OREGON

*

Syzygy: Poems of Essential Theory

Copyright © Brad Dehler 2020, 2025

ALL RIGHTS RESERVED. No part of this work covered by the copyright herein may be reproduced, transmitted, stored, or used in any form or by any means graphic, electronic, or mechanical, including but not limited to photocopying, recording, scanning, digitizing, taping, Web distribution, information networks, or information storage and retrieval systems, except as permitted under Section 107 or 108 of the 1976 United States Copyright Act, without the prior written permission of the author.

Printed in the United States of America
2nd edition

Additional copies are available at
Barnes and Noble
Books-A-Million
Ebay

or www.Amazon.com

For product information, permission to use material from this text, or further permissions questions- please e-mail to: Troika7@gmail.com

---

A special thanks to the formatters at CreateSpace
and for the review and approval from Kindle Direct Publishing KDP
Book design, images and layout: Brad Dehler

ISBN-13: 978-1-966716-02-0
ISBN-10: 1-966716-02-8

Troika Publishng; Salem, Oregon
Printing by KDP/CreateSpace; Charlotte, South Carolina
An Amazon Company
USA

Other Troika Publishng books by Brad Dehler:
Cantus: A Book of Poems
(ISBN-13: 978-0-982-9733-0-1 & ISBN-10: 0-982-97330-6)
http://www.amazon.com/Cantus-Brad-Dehler/dp/0982973306/

Dose: Poems of Quintessential Ethereality
(ISBN-13: 978-0-982-9733-1-8 & ISBN-10: 0-982-97331-4)
https://www.amazon.com/Dose-Quintessential-Ethereality-Brad-Dehler/dp/0982973314

*

"In his work, Brad takes the reader on a soul-searching journey both provocative and intriguing. The choice and use of words, like a fine-tuned instrument elicits an invitation to see beyond the surface. His poetic expressions are a kaleidoscope of life's experiences and desires. There is an honesty about the strength and frailty of the human spirit. The reader can relate to the uncertainty about life and the need for a sense of place and belonging."

-**Kay Loraine** Florence, Oregon
Poetess, decorated Art Therapist, mental health guru & Collagist

*

INTRODUCTION
Syzygy

Welcome to Syzygy. Thank you for choosing this book. This is the third book of poetry in Brad Dehler's repertoire, proceeding the books Cantus & Dose. A syzygy is an event where the sun, earth and moon align; metaphorically a time when we are aligned with our purpose- soul, body and mind. When, not only all is right, but when it is the time most opportune and we are to be ready.

In regards to Troika Studios & Publishng: The vision of a guiding troika arose in Brad's mind while evacuating as a refugee from Hurricane Katrina. He embraced this concept as a driving force, as opposed to a passive beacon, in regards to developing his vocation. The significant reassessment of his location in Past, Present and Future; the use of Poetry, Painting and Drawing in his life -unfurled.

Compared with other poets considered important to any canon- Brad does not pay, in any particular conscious way- attention to traditional use of rhyme, form or literary devices. Rather- the process is very subconscious and kept in very much its raw form. In this way, many trifectas turned triumvirates. Brad feels the importance and believes it is his calling to then share these words of revelation. In hopes they are a light in the dark; leading us through. A tool to help us advance, a foothold to help us grapple. All these things for US, Brad too must heed these challenges and remind himself of mission in compliance with truth. Appreciation, seeking truth- to serve others.

5

SYZYGY
Table of Contents

New Journey	13
Paper Tigers	14
Hunger Was the Life	15
Wine Pairing	16
Every Season	17
Morning Prayer	18
About the Trial	19
Ghost Dance	20
Close the Kingdom	21
Hope they Say	22
Mare Running at Night	23
Soft Soul	24
Your Life is Bigger	25
Cobra on Surfboard	26
Energy Pools	27
Satisfaction is from the Heart	28
It Wasn't a Dream	29
Yearn for Your Gaze	30
Near-Infinite Angles	31
Good River	32
Where the Bullet Lies	33
Scope of Influence	34
How Far is Too Far	35
I Saw the Richat	36
Pole My Decisions	37

*

Words Like Paint	38
All or Nothing	39
Butterfly Will Do the Same	40
Shadows Casted	41
Empty My Hands	42
In Hope We Stride	43
Soaking Fuel Into Soil	44
Sleeper Cell	45
This City	46
Self-Indulgent-Centered	47
Truth Evermore	48
Rebirth	49
Suspended We Grapple	50
For Discipline	51
Tramp Steamer	52
Massage a Bruise	53
Reverse Apparition	54
Modern Trend	55
Divine Light	56
My Mind is Amiss	57
Gut and Heart	58
Troika II	59
What Stars We Are	60
Wonderment Binges	61
Pheno-typicals	62
Sweet Orbiting Outside Myself	63
Shakespeare Labored	64
Entire Room Warmed	65

Artificial Confidence	66
Engaged to a Tombstone	67
Pyres of October	68
As Classical Music	69
Infinite Offense	70
From the Dirty-dirty	71
Let There Be a Gem	72
And True for Prayer	73
Find Peace	74
Death is Imminent	75
Drenched From Years	76
Mitakuye Oyasin	77
Coup of Dove	78
Love is Bigger Than You	79
Sober Days	80
Star-Bird	81
Ideals Up	82
Humility Kick In	83
All Illusion	84
The Forest Changed	85
Wrongs Argued	86
B'The Lake	87
Cross Hatched	88
Title of This Poem Pending Review	89
Cross and Close	90
Love is Alive and Dead	91
My Love from Above	92
Needs Renewal	93

Errror as Mentor	94
Allowance of the Divine	95
Hell Will Compel	96
Scraping Eyes	97
Chasing a Dream	98
Rez Dog	99
A God Among Atheists	100
Shelter Follow Me	101
On the Path	102
Position to Win	103
Medicine Bag	104
What a Dream!	105
Felled Trees	106
Rust Colored Blood	107
Spectating Planets	108
De-Remember	109
Metaphor For Metamorphosis	110
Pennings in Darkness	111
Don't Start Struggling Now	112
Sound Notion	113
Memories are Later	114
To Find Peace	115
Lost My Shirt in the Deal	116
Valley is Low	117
Callous Hands	118
Dog Eat Dog	119
Wait of Time	120
No Reason to Seek	121

*

Sleep in Your Eyes	122
Brad Looks Twice	123
Moving Up on Any Map	124
Unfertile Grotto	125
Shadow Relentlessly Follows	126
Foolhardy Heart	127
Tampering Light	128
Casual Dehumanizing	129
Whimper	130
Diversion from Own Path	131
I Think I Know	132
Dirt in My Hand	133
Regarding Irregardless	134
Path Jagged	135
Knoll in the Plain	136
Scepter-Sword	137
Life Like a Ripcord	138
Cities of Origin	139
Cannot Recall	140
Oft the Latter	141
Magesty of the Human Spirit	142
Forgone Result	143
That Flabbergsted Grey	144
When All I Feel is Spent	145
Without Moderance	146
Ribs Cradle Cryptic Gifts	147
Sleep Be the Thief	148
Razor Burn	149

*

Here is to you
On your new
Heart felt,
    Head bent,
      Liver quenched
Journey

                        Salem 08.20.18

*

Drive into Friday
   Smell the midnight field
Reveal yesterday's
   Sun and Summer shower
Dark road, paper tigers
   Stash pen
Cloud-mountains
Dread the path
Until revelation road

        Modoc Forest, CA 06.25.16

*

Bellies full
Mouths a-grin
Eyes glazed
Over the final course
Hunger was the life

                      Salem 04.12.16

*

Wine pairing with my art
Both subjective
    Of varied flavor
So give more wine
To the subject
To solicit favor

                    Salem 5.18.14 @0124

*

Repeat Repentance
Because it is in our nature
Need for reminding
Renewal every season

        Gardnerville, NV 06.26.16

*

Bless the clients
Bless this house of counsel
And bless me
    The clinician

                      Salem 2017

*

So many ways to convey
I am sure you are relieved
    About the trial
The judge was mistaken
Jury confused
Are you relieved?
Wrong decision, good outcome
Good decision, good for you
Bad for society

Prison in decision
Prison indecision

                        Salem 10.09.19

*

The coming summer shower
In the Mesmer ozone
Blurred headdress motioned
Ghost dance with
Crow primaries
On hallowed ground
Ancestors lost
We seek gain; a living

        Modoc Forest, CA 06.26.16

*

How close the kingdom
Roles be blessed
Royal aspiration pushes away
    Pushing off of
Though kingdom is in your name
Ancestors take your namesake
Close indeed, kingdom inside you

                    Salem 06.26.18

*

I hope they say
'You brought brightness
   and light'
To the perimeters
And clarity to the core

                    Salem 07.10.19 @1402

*

A mare running at night
Ominous omens surrounding me
A mayor running in delight
No good coming from this
Representative of only yourself

                Eugene, OR 05.24.19

*

Hardened heart
    To protect
Your soft soul
Self-sabotage vs sacrifice
The peril
Of survive
Over thrive

                    Salem 05.20.16

*

Focus on the Truth
Rather than patents
Or other refinements
Your Life
    Is bigger than you

                        Salem 09.25.19

*

Cobra on surfboard
Find your center
Align heart over center
Head over heart
All in order
Heart over everything
In the present
Head for the future
Gutted in the past
As well as for reflex
Focus on your breath

                         Bend, Oregon 10.08.16

*

Rivers- good and necessary
But where is your lake?
Where your ocean
Where this energy pools
Defines your depths

                        Salem 12.04.16

*

Satisfaction is from the heart
Dislocated in things
There is always
The possibility of
Dissatisfaction
Thinking 'one more'
'Something new'
Mind is insatiable
Devour knowledge
Thin line of aggrandizement
And enhancement

                        Salem 10.20.17

It wasn't a dream
It was a vague memory
From my fickle mind
Over tricky fingers
And slighted hands
Having trouble tracking
No, it wasn't a dream

                        Salem 08.12.2020

*

Bless my attention
En route to understanding
Comprehension of urgency
    And
Not to forget memory
I yearn for your gaze
Please that look
    Upon me with favor
To listen, please teach
In other words, sanctify

                  Castle Rock, WA 03.03.17

*

Before I was told about the ways
I was talking to eternity
We live in a world
    Of near-infinite angles
    From point to point
The possibilities confound us
Infinite from
    Our inability to process

                  Salem 10.30.17

*

Good river
Flow with liquid force

Good or bad
Experience merges with our being
Accused of running away
   Or hiding
Perhaps some are cleansing
   And starting anew

                       Salem 03.03.18

*

The truth where the bullet lies
Or where it has gone through
Critical origin
"Why fret"
The bullet no longer in you
"It's over"
It's not

                        Salem 01.20.2020

*

Accepting dirt on your hands
Contaminates your inner being
You now see it on you
Then corrupted your thoughts

Do not be preoccupied
Lest you consumed
Do not belittle
    Your scope of influence
They need you
If abandoned for personal glory
    You fail all

   St Sharbel Portland, OR 03.05.17

*

How far is too far
Where we draw the line
Sometimes
Count the ways
Count the days
A million blinks
Or a single life

                Salem 04.16.18

*

I saw the Richat
It looked back
I could now see
In me
What I could not see
Previously

                       Salem 03.06.2020

*

If only I could pull
Andy Warhol into the discussion
Yet more from Thomas
Aquinas dissertation
If only I could poll my decisions
If only I could pull
In-from the heavens

        Salem 04.23.2020 @ 0139

*

Rhyme words like paint
Clash bad
Bright and inviting attractive
Able to coat to appear
    Two things are alike

                Castlerock, WA 11.04.17

*

It's all or nothing
Happens every time
Followed you to
    The threshold twice
The wound is gushing

                Salem 12.30.15

*

They always
Say
Like a moth to a flame
But a butterfly
Will do the same

                                Salem 05.11.16

*

Shadows are not born
They are casted
Existing because
    There is a light source

                        Salem 08.27.19

*

There are things I must lay down
    Now
Things I carried
To enable my trek here
But now I empty my hands
To grasp my new objective

                Salem 08.06.2020 @0234

*

We are on the edge of the world
Reconciliation is a map back
Hour of our death
Mile-marker
In hope we stride
In stride we heal

        Castlerock, WA 11.04.17

*

Soaking fuel into soil
Render both useless
To our need
Prayer chain smokers
Hoboken chokin'
Dimming twilight stage
   Of life

                    Salem 10.16.16

*

Inside us all
That sleeper cell
That accepted dose of poison
Far more unstable
    Than our facades let on
Then there is the one
That cracks or explodes
We find our decoy

                  Salem 10.14.19 @0203

*

This city
It breaks you
It makes you
    Want to fold
Guilt gilded on you
Grace may be hastened from you
Heart of gold
Silver soul
Mettle of your mind to keep it
    All together

                Seattle, WA 07.15.18 @1238

*

The self-indulgent-centered
Ask of many things

The one predictor
Inquire
    About wants and needs

                  Salem 11.12.17

*

Often we have stories
By storytellers
Who have agendas
What happens to truth
When the one with true memory
Passes
    And
The remnants of false remain
Assuredly
There is the truth
Evermore. Unchanged

                                     Salem 04.29.18

*

Boy to juvenile to man
To family father
Rebirth

                        Salem 08.12.18

*

I reach my art
Pumping blood
My song my paint
My charcoal my poems
I recognize yours
You reject mine
I reject you
You reject me

And separate we float

Suspended- we grapple
    We are grounded
When we gravitate to good
Our stories again intermingle
What is mine is ours

                      Salem 08.12.18

*

Talk of selling album blank
Shows that it has
    The same message
Nothing
May you keep admiration
    For discipline
May all your doubts
    Remain curious
All your good will
Hopeful

                Grand Ronde, OR 08.24.18

*

Catch a random ride
On a tramp steamer
Spontaneous on my balms
Dispersing dollars by palm
Pushing my perspective
Then
Relaxed
Rolling back
On hindfoot for healing

                Salem 02.19.19 @0123

*

Massage a bruise
Will not comfort the discomforted
I'll sing the same song
The same way
For my own recognition

                      Salem 08.24.19

*

Perhaps we are the ghosts of
The reverse apparition
The flinch image
The flicker in the mirror

                    Salem 11.26.18

*

Modern trend
Is the further separating
    The terms
Grievous and egregious

                      Salem 11.06.16

*

Shine upon me thy divine light
Whose gentle rays harass darkness
The present tense of
Won is win
One is when
If I could have been there
In that moment of devastation
As you are
Now, as you were
Belief you are nothing
Lost worth
Though in pursuit of truth
I can see your pain
By your display
In your art or anger
I can hold it for ransom
Until your return

                    Castle Rock, WA 02.02.19

*

Been howling at the moon
Discontented
No body hearing
Cried out the side
Of my eyes

My mind is amiss
My soul an abyss
But all goodness
Makes it a plentiful receptor
That much more
To hold graces

                              Salem 10.12.18

*

Resemblance is not mimicry
Our trunk resembles a snake
Contains our gut and heart

                      Salem 09.07.19

*

```
Troika
The two horses
Of which I am aware
    Driving
Dark horse
    Takes lead
Least considered
```

                            Salem 09.07.19

*

You ask what stars we are
Beyond mere celebrity
Gaze into the deep black beyond
Contrasted by their glimmer
We traveled far
To now be near each other
So the stars we are
Not the ones in similar proximity
But
The two brightest close
    In counterbalance

        Pacific City, OR Summer 2000

*

Every day is a new day
Until it is not
A new day old from routine
Ripe for retirement
On that pathway, hinges
Your wonderment binges
    Of fanciful fruit
Possibilities plucked, glimmering

                    Salem 05.26.16

*

Grudge held
Being wronged was whitewashed
Across all pheno-typicals
You are going to die
By the bite
Of your ancestors

                      Salem 10.18.19 @0739

*

The ethyl center of the
    Milky Way
Raspberry rum on the tongue
Pull me outside my centeredness
The barycenter
Sweet orbiting outside myself

                      Salem 09.16.16

*

Shakespeare labored
To explain our kind of love

Salem 10.12.16

*

I find solace in the cry room
Despite- I am not crying
Entire room warmed
    By my presence
Faithfulness for the faithless
Goodness without witness
Reduction of God to bite size
Morsel enough (Save you)
Affliction avoided by infliction
(Bathe you)
Scar bestowed
Asleep, I was caught in the wake

                Newport, OR 11.09.19

*

Sure as unpredictable is
I lost it all in my mind
Confidence is artificial
Until it lays impression
Slays doubt

                        Salem 04.06.17

*

As foolish to be
    Engaged with a tombstone
Than in conversation
    With a fool

                        Salem 10.12.16

*

The pyres of October
Alit in November
Led to Embers
   By December's end
Now why do we tremble
In this season's preamble
From plight
   Of winter's frozen night
Or the bon fire
May turn
   To conflagration
(Pyro) pyrrhic victories
Here ye; Hear-see
We need warmth, give us shelter

Here-say
Months of dismay

                        Salem 10.20.16

*

She is beautiful
As classical music
Surrounding me
With a lovely string piece

                      Salem 06.19.19

*

Infinite offense against
An infinite soul
A child abandoned
A man never known

                    Salem 02.14.17

*

We reckless
We sightless
From the dirty-dirty
You heard me
You're sure to get shot
Triggers rep a rap sheet
Just as long as your block

                New Orleans 2004

*

When supply is low
The leftovers low quality
When we are in deprivation
Please good shepherd
Good current guiding
Let there be a gem

                        Salem 09.18.16

*

Proceeding through
Half-hearted
Renders one resentful
Be it
    Cadet not to be police
    Artist not fully realized
    Sportsman only dreaming
And true for prayer

                Salem 06.02.2020 @2020

*

How can one find peace
When one has lost
   So many pieces

                     Salem 06.21.17 @2122

Death is imminent
Just around the coroner

                Salem 05.14.2020 @1202

*

Flesh lays on my face
Will eventually droop
Drenched from years

                Hill AFB, Utah 1998

*

Let us speak in direct lines
Avoidant of seductive
    Curved, pleasantries
Let us appreciate what we are
    What we have
And put to best use
To become all we can
So we say
Mitakuye Oyasin

                Salem 01.15.18 @1940

*

Claim to be a dove
Calling "coup, coup"
Warhawk semantic mimicry
Shift away from populous
    Chicken coop. Pituitary
Lie when you rest
Stand where you are

                          Salem 10.15.19

*

Love is bigger than you
Love your husband,
Your wife,
Your sister,
Your brother,
Love your father,
Your mother
Love before yourself
Love is capitalized
You put after love
    Love is
Love within yourself, then
Your love can
Exist in a multitude
    Of others
Beyond self

                      Portland, OR 04.01.12

*

The sober days are
Numbered days
The somber days are
Over days
The tortured days
Are nights

                        Salem 10.16.19

*

Star-bird
Love written word
But comfortably in the sand
Perched on right hand
Like Phoenix but without death
Coo dove gentle breath
Need not resurrect
Rest, now, with me here
Pardon as I bend your ear
Recompense
Patient for me
I will return as a listener
Parallel, disarming
Blissfully in the ether
Present- my heart

                Salem 01.20.2020

Ideals
Up for attack
Far more for guilt
Than inadequacy

                Portland, OR 09.11.09

*

Note some humility
Kick in
Beware the ego
Kick out

                        Salem 06.20.16

*

You say
'There is no time'
Did you mean
Time ran out
Time is up
Or
Never there was
    All illusion

                Salem 03.16.2020 @2323

*

The forest changed
But slower than the ocean shore
Recognizable for long
    Stints of time
You are like the ocean
Your personality makes
So that I do not
    Really know you
The ebb and flow of tides
Shaped you strangely

                        Newport, OR 01.27.19

*

The wrongs will be
Argued through the night
For none concerned
The right

                        Salem 07.12.16

*

A home in the wood
As well as b'the lake
B'the bridge
Heart b'the head
Feel my hand in the dark

                      Salem 05.15.19

Cross hatched shady plan

Salem 09.28.18

*

For as long as I'm short with you

Salem 05.19.18

*

I cross my heart
And
Close my eyes

                                      Salem 10.17.17

*

Love is alive and dead
Dead when dead in you
Love for life
Alive and well
When love exalted
Marriage- fidelity to that
Never compromising
That which you
    Protect with all your being
That is how it is greater
Than our flawed humanity

                      Portland, OR 09.11.09

*

Better be better to me
Better be better than me
The youth stands on the
    Sturdy father's shoulders
Driven by mother's nurturance
Thinking of
My love from above

                  Salem 07.17.2020 @2355

*

Love is only for a moment
Then needs renewal
In between
    The bliss so sweet
And Dedication
When conflict
Afflicts us

                      Salem 04.05.18

*

When sole reliance
On experience
    To guide you
You accept error
As mentor

                    Salem 10.06.08

*

What is holiness or hedonism
    Without help
Heaven
Whispers condemned to intention
Or elevated to assertiveness
Prayers ascend us
By at least calibrating the mind
All the way
To the allowance of the divine

                Vancouver, WA 11.17.18

*

Dread if Heaven
Cannot help
Hell will compel

                        Salem 08.02.16

*

The contacts between the lines
That lies between the lies
The truth between our minds
Scraping eyes
With Satan

                        Salem 09.20.18

*

Chasing a dream
Running from yourself
With hopes
That self and dream
    Merge
At the place of dreams
Please not Oneirophrenia

                  Salem 12.06.19

I am just a downed-luck
Rez dog
Stranded on this land
    Allotted to me
From nomad
To force-fed

                        Portland, OR 2010

*

A god among atheists
The God
A/The -ists
Impressed by self, leaves
    No room for impressions
Raptured within being

					Salem 04.23.2020

*

Shelter follow me
Food nourish me
Clothing enwrap me
Love reign within me

                          Salem 10.11.18

*

On the path to holiness
It is beyond dirt capabilities
It is that owl perched
    High above
    Yet connected
We must seek forward
Unfocused, feel inadequate
Precarious
Misinterpreted,
    Pull for betterment
Calibration to that path

                Salem 01.12.17 @0859

*

I am in a position
To win
    Because I have been
In a disposition
Of loss

                  Salem 02.22.2020

*

Medicine bag
Hangs around neck
Next to heart

                       Portland, OR 01.17.17

*

Oh!
What a dream
It's been
To be alive

                        Salem 08.10.16

*

Felled trees
That propelled our dreams
Which united schemes
And hailed pleas
Hallowed out of ice
That revolved thrice
Which burned the patience
And defined our station

                    Salem 03.30.16

*

Rust colored blood
Cannot save it 'til I'm done
Got to rush, got to gun
Sparkles as it runs
Flat tone as it dries
Darkens as I die

                    Salem 08.14.19

*

Spectating planets
Through our own atmosphere
Staid life
Stay woke
There is trauma
It is an emergency
Don't close your eyes
They may not reopen
That zone
    Became a limit

                        Salem 09.26.19

*

Re remember
Deremember
De-December
At the end of the cycle
Do not dismember
Ripe and ready rendered

                        Salem 03.14.18

*

Metaphor for metamorphosis
Abounds
Sought meaning
In the queries
Quandaries footed quagmire

                      Salem 11.04.19

*

The sun up in grand entry
Magnificent again in setting
In between
    My pennings in darkness
I hold out for next light
I promise to later
    Pay off my sleep debt
All still in the oranges
Striated with wispy cloud
Resolution fulfilled in honoring
Each glorious morn & retirement

                        Salem 03.24.19

*

Don't start struggling now
I need you
I need you- I need you
Don't start struggling now
I got my hands on the wheel
But my eyes misread
Don't touch struggling now
The lyrics come to
    I sing to myself
Don't start struggling now
Dropping into the mire
    And
I'm two feet deep
Struggling now
    I tell myself
While I fear the worst

                        Salem 03.06.2020

*

Let us not lose sight
Of the sound notion
To forage the food within grasp
But I look past the glass
To a bigger world
I cannot reach it
But it is my tale to share
Conceiving of things
Realized and fulfilled
Without yet beyond bound

                        Salem 05.27.2020 @0127

*

What does it take
To take a moment
In waves rolling over you
Still external

Breathe deep. Take five.
Hang five
Hold a pose
That you can propose later
Take a stance
    To return
To this circumstance
Never to be recreated
Do not fool yourself
Now is now
Memories are later

                        Newport, OR 01.25.19

*

To find sanctuary
To find peace
Go to Salem,
   OR
Go to Solemn, Mass.

                        Salem 05.20.2020

*

I lost my shirt in the deal
Yay the hanger holds my place

Salem 08.24.19

*

My hope is high
Though my luck is low
My well is dry
Though the valley shadowed
Though the valley is low

        Dallas, TX 09.20.05 @0950

*

Callous hands
To handle more
Tolerance in adversity
So that experience is gainful

                        Salem 08.10.18

*

In this dog eat dog
Rat race
Or frog versus frog
World- however you perceive it
I'm not a consumable

                      Salem 09.10.19

*

Eyes not foreseeing
The wait of time
Over the seeming ton of years
Been a long winter
In this hinterland
Yore lore golden
Classic music plays
In my newfound transition

                              Salem 03.02.16

*

Any other woman but you
An other woman
Another woman
There is no reason to seek
Any woman other than you

   Flower Mound, TX 09.18.05 @0200

*

Doing regrettable things-
Sleep in your eyes

                                        Salem 01.18.19

Brad Looks Twice
One muddy, rocky road
One smooth paved road
The poor -tough down the rocky
Muddy if caught in the turmoil
The ease of the smooth
Delivers one soft and content
The one
I would not wish upon
Anyone

           Salem 05.29.2020 @1034

*

When feeling down
Keep moving forward
That Way
Moving up
On any map

                Salem 12.20.19

*

```
Unfertile grotto
    Of Adonis
Let us escape
Jettison- out route
God writes straight
On crooked lines
```

    Covington, LA May 2004

*

I tread in silence
Not to assume
    Or indict
    Nor indicate
    To acquit
    Or vindicate
Still the shadow
Relentlessly follows
And the smoke chases me
Faulty memory displaces me
Challenging devotion
    To my creed

                         Salem 01.11.08

*

Foolhardy foolish heart
Quakes tempest
Shakes my vessel
Born mortally wounded
Fundamental problem
Onward we struggle

                          Salem 07.01.18

*

They made hobbyist of my heart
Collector of my bones
Soothsayer of my habits
Beacon to my faults
Soliciting silence by what shone

Temperate light moderately posed
Tempering light strong exposure
Only tampering light pre-exposed

                        Salem 11.26.16

*

Problematic in casual
    Dehumanizing
Depersonalization
Did she give birth
    To a boy or to her son?
Give birth to a girl
    Or to the world?
Liable am I now

                Salem 04.23.2020 @0119

*

Whimper
Think you are the victim?
World coming to an end?
Plead for psychiatry
Excusing your sins for disease
Look unto yourself
Better make a check

                Travis AFB, CA 07.21.1994

*

Live and teach
Upon the one true path
But do not wait in idle
    Expectation
Leave result to trust
For a man will resist diversion
    From his own path
To honor his own choice

                    Salem 12.17.07

*

```
I think
I know this
This I know
I think I know
I feel
I feel I know
I know I feel,
   I think
```

                          Salem 03.19.19 @0249

*

I want to reconnect
With the world
The object that gets me
That much closer to the heavens
From my personal abyss
Sit and look
At the dirt in my hand
As I did in youth

                        Salem 07.26.19

*

No matter the platform
    On which you stand
Irregardless of your
    Perceived power
Regardless of your
    Own weight
You cannot lift yourself
    Up with your platform

                    Salem 04.13.11

*

My path has been jagged
The rains ceaseless
Every move is aching
I lament my discarded trust
Invested in a world
    Where now
The only kind of peace known
Is Death

                    Salem 03.15.11

*

In the big broad plain
Things look all alone
Stay by my side
I will show you home
I will show you past
    This grassy knoll
Tune the noise to harmony
It's the dust
    That shows your past
It's the waste
    That attracts the rats
My swollen feet mock surprise
Journey for a cure
    Got healed along the way

                Travis AFB, CA 07.09.1996

*

Quick- tell us a story of triumph
Many have there been times
Of affliction, war, forlorn
Now is the era
To open our narrow scope
We are on the edge of despair
Charge forward with torches
Leading with scepter-sword

                      Salem 07.29.08

*

My life is
Like a ripcord
Done in a flash
Apogee
Effigy
Refugee

                    Salem 03.16.2020

*

Your cities of origin
Fail you
Miscreants froth from settlers
Go to soil fed roots
Red dirt
Shaping clay

                Salem 08.18.20 @0140

*

Short is my sleep
I cannot recall my dreams

                    Salem 07.12.19

*

Serve me or fail me
My memory oft the latter

                              Salem 02.09.19

Hope that these words
Look you in the eyes
Becoming composition
From provocative words
Nearing the majesty
    Of the human spirit
That presence
    In Person

Pleading in the second stanza
Challenging desire
Mind grind
Path of destruction

Learn the dangers of the wild
Wandering away
But within the wild, safe
Beside a beast

                    Salem 06.29.19

*

Foregone result
When knocked on your back
Tears flow
To the ears
When facing trauma
Remaining standing
Tears flow to the mouth

                Salem 05.30.15

*

That flabbergasted gray
"They are killers"
"Everyone's a killer"
Blend metaphors
Demote change
Promote apathy
Destroy meaning
That flabbergasted grey

                Salem 04.13.2020 @1009

*

Dissent or assent
Descend or ascend
When all I feel is spent
Crooked eyes bent
Unlifted for compassion
When the culled passion isn't.
All I know is I am sent

                Salem 05.07.2020

*

Without moderance
Pleasures become vices
For some, once is excess
Paid too much for that price tag

                    Salem 10.03.08

*

My ribs cradle
   Cryptic gifts
Parochial in my sickness
I am vitalized
I know about the
   50-pound halo
All this sanctifying
Starvation preying on my mind
I am a deadbeat father
Of the 3rd world countries

        Fairfield, CA 05.26.1996

*

Though sleep be the thief
Of my consciousness
I want you beside me

                    Albany, OR 02.16.03

*

It's that razor burn
Chance to learn
It's that winced morning
Fair warning
Avoidance of
The catastrophic eve

                    Salem 07.09.19

THIS PAGE INTENTIONALLY LEFT BLANK

Port Tree
Poe Tree
Poe In Tre
Poor Tree
Paw Tree
Pawtry
Tawdry
Opoetry
Oetry
Put try
Poor Try
Po Dry
Poedry
Potry potpourri
Poet y
Poe It Try
Poet Ree
Pot Ree
Struck by the Ree
Poe in Salem
P03
POE
Po Etty
Poa-try
Pour-try
Pour-tri

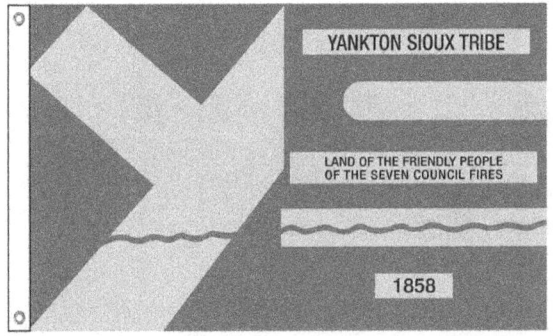

Cantus: A Book of Poems
Paperback ISBN-13: 978-0-982-9733-0-1 & ISBN-10: 0-982-97330-6
Hardcover ISBN: 978-0-982-9733-3-2
Paperback (5x8) ISBN-13: 978-1-966716-00-6 & ISBN-10: 1-966716-00-1
http://www.amazon.com/Cantus-Brad-Dehler/dp/0982973306/

Dose: Poems of Quintessential Ethereality
Paperback ISBN-13: 978-0-982-9733-1-8 & ISBN-10: 0-982-97331-4
Hardcover ISBN: 978-0-982-9733-4-9
Paperback (5x8) ISBN-13: 978-1-966716-01-3 & ISBN-10: 1-966716-01-X
https://www.amazon.com/Dose-Quintessential-Ethereality-Brad-Dehler/dp/0982973314

Syzygy: Poems of Essential Theory
Paperback ISBN-13: 978-0-982-9733-2-5 & ISBN-10: 0-982-97332-2
Hardcover ISBN: 978-0-982-9733-5-6
Paperback (5x8) ISBN-13: 978-1-966716-02-0 & ISBN-10: 1-966716-02-8
https://www.amazon.com/Syzygy-Essential-Theory-Brad-Dehler/dp/0982973322

Shadow Catching: Poems of Existential Peering
Paperback ISBN-13: 978-0-982-9733-6-3 & ISBN-10: 0-982-97336-5
Hardcover ISBN: 978-0-982-9733-7-0
Paperback (5x8) ISBN-13: 978-1-966716-03-7 & ISBN-10: 1-966716-03-6
https://www.amazon.com/Shadow-Catching-Poems-Existential-Peering-Brad-Dehler/dp/B0BMY5M9CN

Epiphaneia: Lost Poems of Epistemological Endeavor
Paperback (5x8) ISBN-13: 978-0-982-9733-8-7 & ISBN-10: 0-9829733-8-1
Hardcover ISBN: 978-0-982-9733-9-4
https://www.amazon.com/Epiphaneia-Lost-Poems-Epistemological-Endeavor/dp/0982973381

SHADOW CATCHING

**Poems of
Existential Peering**

Brad Dehler

TROIKA STUDIOS & PUBLISHNG
SALEM, OREGON

Shadow Catching: Poems of Existential Peering

Copyright © Brad Dehler 2022, 2025

ALL RIGHTS RESERVED. No part of this work covered by the copyright herein may be reproduced, transmitted, stored, or used in any form or by any means graphic, electronic, or mechanical, including but not limited to photocopying, recording, scanning, digitizing, taping, Web distribution, information networks, or information storage and retrieval systems, except as permitted under Section 107 or 108 of the 1976 United States Copyright Act, without the prior written permission of the author.

Printed in the United States of America
2nd edition

Additional copies are available at
Barnes and Noble // Books-A-Million
Booktopia.com.au // Ebay // Thriftbooks
Abebooks.com // Goodreads.com // WritersCafe
Betterworldbooks.com // Duckscottage.com
or www.Amazon.com

For product information, permission to use material from
this text, or further permissions questions- please e-mail to:
Troika7@gmail.com

A special thanks to the formatters at CreateSpace
and to the details, content, and quality reviewers from Kindle Direct Publishing KDP
A Book of Bard; Poemadeh candidate

ISBN-13: 978-1-966716-03-7 & ISBN-10: 1-966716-03-6
Hardcover ISBN: 978-0-9829733-7-0

Troika Studios & Publishing; Salem, Oregon
Printing by KDP/CreateSpace; Charlotte, South Carolina
An Amazon Company
USA

"The book "Syzygy" written by Brad Dehler is almost thirty years of lessons, thoughts, questions and learning to understand the meaning of being alive. The poetry reflects the movement of our world. Sometimes we understand and sometimes, we do not. Some of the poetry is brutally honest and some of the poetry is gentle and kind. The writer takes us on a ride grasping at hope, his books plunge you to many places and into many lessons. You must read again to catch the hidden wisdom. I recommend the books- which are to be re-read, to find solid ground in complexity."

- **John Castellenas "Coyote": Michigan Poet.** Published by Poetry Soup, Short-Edition, Poem Hunter, Writer's Café, among other sources.

"I like this poetry of Brad Dehler. No mean feat to write so incisively and succinctly. Intricate and lyrical. Brilliant."

-Davey Payne: Poet of Dumfries, Scotland

"Speechless. Amazing, great poetry. "We are the shore of something great" > amazing wisdom within such imagery. Really good poetry.... genuine, direct and concise- with perfect sense of math and metric. I humbly bow, sincerely."

-Amber Stone: Nepali-English Poet; "Just a loving work in progress", Poetry 101 Member

3

INTRODUCTION
Shadow Catching

Shadow Catching is the fourth book written by Brad Dehler; proceeding the books Cantus, Dose & Syzygy. Syzygy was released in the year 2020 when Brad Dehler asserted that it was a year of 'clear vision' prior to the start of the year. It was not foreseen how apropos this notion was in considering how our eyes have opened up to the overreach of those in power. Dose is the second book (the "dos" book written) which explores art and poetry as medicine (as in a dose of medicine). Cantus is aptly named as the initial song, initial book as it was projecting this inspired style of poetry. In reference of Troika Studios and Publishng, the troika represents that unfailing driving force before, during and after most difficult challenges. While at the same time, a trifecta as the avenue for success.

The title of this book: 'Shadow Catching', refers to Brad's Indian name bestowed upon him by his late beloved grandmother Lilly who taught about his ancestors, history and Sioux native ways. Ancestors who have since been relegated to Rosebud Reservation in particular and other surrounding reservations.

This book is an example of how a few mysteries may be deciphered from the world around us. A way of hunting and trapping some enigmas. While some poems are complete puzzles to be identified and appreciated (in this book Shadow Catching), some

are individual pieces with puzzle edges showing-
there is more to explore. These are to further
thought processing and discussion in an open-
ended fashion. In addressing how these poems
arise; it seems as an inspiration, divine spark
sent for perspective and ultimately a development
of obligation and relation to Truth.

These poems float solo, not part of a larger
constructed story and not for personal
aggrandizement. Sometimes serious of nature, at
other times in levity. Promote these with
patience in your own thoughts. Perhaps there are
solutions & may they be helpful to you. There is
potential to elevate some prayerfully; if so-
would be so blessed by you.

This is an attempt to share the goodness in
publishing these poems. I am not claiming to be a
master of it. It is more of the "what is to be
done" and not so much the "how" until the reader
processes. Why? It is for you to decipher.
The who is you, I, us.

Shadow Catching
Table of Contents

Bloodlines	15
Trenches Carved	16
Conflict Resolution	17
Return Home Another Way	18
The Mind Balks	19
Traveler Along the Way	20
See Red; Redemption	21
There is a Home for It	22
Something Happened Out There	23
Retirement of the Facts	24
One is the Other	25
Acid Rain in Alkali Lakes	26
Faux Gold	27
Room Running Short	28
Eternal Essence of Beauty	29
Premarital Hex	30
Acronym of My Fate	31
Sitting By Myself	32
Money Clip	33
Not Really Sad	34
Straight-Away Visions	35
Grammar Grammer	36
Seminole Spirit	37
Awoke in it's Wake	38

To Love, Whole Heart	39
Filter Through Pilgramage	40
People Tend Towards	41
Truth Touches All	42
Eddie Ate Dynomite	43
Go to Slaughter	44
Awaken in the Ride	45
Overcast Blocks My Stars	46
Hand of My Ancestor	47
Not Enough	48
Long Addiction	49
Relationship with the Eternal	50
That Day	51
Tail Pitched High	52
Common Confines	53
More to be Said	54
Because We Can	55
Who Are Victorious	56
Deed You Well	57
In the Middle	58
Annexation of Peace	59
Push the Hours	60
Pair of Bull	61
Negative Example	62
In One Rendezvous	63
Darkest Shadows	64
In the Same Age	65
Walking Wounded	66

If Our Creator was Chaos	67
Tolling of the Bell	68
Dominate in Our Domicile	69
Yet Irreversible	70
On Way to Opus	71
Estranged By Distance	72
Fall on My Sword	73
Every Angler	74
Only Way for Help	75
Reversal of Fortune	76
Sioux-Side	77
I am Tender	78
Future Flawed	79
E-V'er Junior	80
Peace on the Line	81
Brushes with Death	82
Term of Art	83
Hear-Say Heresy	84
That was Your Guide	85
Prayer Powerful	86
Mission in Our Direction	87
Freedom and Salvation	88
Identity	89
I Eminate Me	90
Children at Play	91
Nakota Where-House	92
Put an Eye On That	93
Surreal Disorientation	94

Sympathize Hypocrisy	95
People in Boat	96
Arrow with a Point	97
Verbatim	98
Told Them to Refrain	99
We Share Orbit	100
Blackest Black	101
Red Eye Flight	102
Call Their Name	103
Bromides Vs Bona Fides	104
Continued Into the Heavens	105
Good Hunger	106
Give Me Some More	107
Numerous Rings	108
Led Into Battle	109
Carry On Your Name	110
Father, Son, Husband, Holy Ghost	111
White Light	112
Act of God or Governor	113
Better than Nothing	114
Off Right	115
Feel My Fate	116
A Certain Tide	117
Option	118
Gatekeeper	119
More Than an Effigy	120
Celestial Particulate	121
Rare Breed	122

Precipice of Faith	123
Facets of the One	124
If Let-Left to Fester	125
Paid Accolades	126
Blot it All Out Black	127
In Complete Control	128
Point of No Return	129
Good Work Rained Down	130
Better This Way	131
Water Warms in Hand	132
One Degree	133
Pressure, Pressure!	134
The Body is Rain	135
Sightless Eyespots	136
Intently Inhale	137

*

Bloodlines
Lay down talk of quantums
Back to Running Bull
    Still running
Sitting Bull
    Still sitting
Red Cloud
    Still elevating
We share the same blood
Oneness
Like the connection
Of vehicle and bridge
Different material
In the same cause
Cross over, we track it
Or the same pause
Arrow to target

                                  Salem 09.13.21

*

```
Trenches carved
     By our walk
Forming our path
     Warming our expectation
The trenches we dig
     Devise our defense
     Secures our safety
```

          Salem 09.12.21

Conflict Resolution
More like mending fences
Save face
Able to retreat without disgrace
    Than compromise
    And seeing eye to eye
Giving those doubts
    A proper burial
False concepts fall
Not only when pushed
But with the woken dreamer

                Salem 07.30.2020 @2348

*

Frankincense of otherworldliness
I visit from afar
Bringing soil, water and air
Since I could not capture the air
I come to you with
My breath of representation
Having this impact here, wiser
I return home another way

                    Silver Lake, OR 01.03.21

*

The mind balks
Before it boggles

                        Salem 06.16.21

*

```
Trilling down the embarcadero
Take right
On 100 Souls Road
Traveler along the way
Ever rolling
     Never rest
Not a passer-by
     Be blessed
Stop only to help the distressed
```

                        Jerome, ID 08.19.22 @0433

*

There is no see red;
    Redemption
There is only sea red;
    Insatiable appetite

        Salem 09.25.18

*

Trust me
There is a home for it
I will put
    A structure around you
Comfort and protect you
Shelter and amuse you
Your aching head
Tortured heart
There is a home for it
With me

                  Salem 06.30.20 @1322

*

Something happened out there
In California
Amongst the waves
Of the deepening ocean
Seaside abodes falling
For its shifting border
Away from the burning acres
Something happened on the streets
Of the projects
Started righting
Writing the wrongs
Something one in the same
Or something very different

                                              Salem 04.02.21

*

There is no simple
Retirement of the facts
Every conclusion
Leads down a certain road

                        Salem 12.23.19

*

Life is life
Death is death
Troubled by iniquities
When confused on that point
When life imitates death
Or death-life
Authentication then confounding
One is the other

                    Rockaway Beach, OR 08.28.21

*

Was the west won
Or did it lose it's shooters?
I scrape across the barren desert
I see dry creek beds
Stark playas
Learn their seasonal quench
Acid rain in alkali lakes
To see past my own fraud
Inexplicable miracle
But once done
I had to live a different life

                        Salem 09.11.2020 @0035

*

I was told it was faux gold
I gave it away
So it wouldn't be fools gold
Second guess- my second impression
Realizing scam
Now seeing it foe's gold

                          Salem 09.11.2020 @ 0833

*

I get the feeling
We are all in
A room running short of oxygen
You do not hold
    Your head down
You do not bother
    To lift

                        Corvallis, OR 11.20.98

*

Eternal essence of beauty
Ironic for the word
Be it fleeting here
Perhaps not so magical
    As we hoped
Second look at quaking aspen
Exemption by example

                          Salem 01.01.19 @1811

*

Premarital hex
Fly too close to the sun
Icarus wax poetic
Pleas old desire
New gravity deaf
Fall, breaks union

                    Oakridge, OR 12.10.2021

*

Browning, Poe, Dickinson
Acronym of my fate
Acrimonious if disputed
Initials of my sake
Imbibe yet never reconstituted
Be with me now
Read and ravish allegory

                                      Salem   07.25.2020

*

I was sitting by myself
Not within myself

                        Salem 07.25.2020

*

What was that?
I forethought
The losing of the money clip
Back before Albuquerque
At that time
    I dismissed it as fear
    Loss of a valuable
Now it seems
More premonition
Losing item
    Gaining clairvoyance
Post facto

                    Odessa, Texas 08.21.22 @0222

*

If only
We could discard
Our iniquities to the dirt
It's complex
To my simple mind
In reality, simple in itself
I'm not really sad

                       Salem 07.25.20

*

```
We get trapped
In our straight-away visions
Forward facing
First person perspective
Speeding down our roadway
As our sights
    Blurred in the periphery
We collide with each other
En masse
```

  Deschutes Forest, OR 12.11.21 @ 1219

*

The sacrificial lamb
The disadvantaged friend
The one whom you feel
    Smarter than
Grammar
The one you feel smarter, then
Every little gram counted
Grammer
Pride suspended alone

                      Salem 03.07.18

*

Seminole spirit
Fend off opposition
Hope prevailing over termination
Refusing to
    Negotiate our demise
Red Cloud hung over us
Crazy Horse held out
By bone and blood Little Bighorn
It's a third world country
Out there
    Where I have been removed
Place of my abandon
    Where I relinquish
    My reluctance
Now, into the Black Hills

                        Seminole, Texas 08.20.22

*

Invigorated by the ocean
Awoke in its wake
Inevitable I return to land
This time will tide me over

                        Salem 07.23.20

*

To Love, whole heart
To hate, hole heart
They say there's a
    God-shaped hole
Remaining to fill
Consuming black hole dwarfed
To the celestial whole

                                    Salem 06.25.20

*

Lie through teeth
Teeth not a filter
Snarling, biting
Dense, deflecting
Filter through pilgrimage
Highway 90 flushing air
Wind left behind us

                    Albany, OR 01.01.22

*

There are many things
People tend towards
Tend to be selfish
Trend towards populous
Tend towards fear
All disguised
What we pretend to be

                                      Salem 11.28.21

*

Not an impression
It is inclination
That there is something
Undiscovered, more, unknown tell
Of justice
Truth touches all
But does not reside in all

                    Gilchrist, OR 06.06.21

Eddie Ate Dynamite
Good Bye Eddie
Mnemonic guitar playing
Strings to disaster
Minus Eddie

                                          Salem 07.11.19

*

Brisk cold morning
Produced brisk walk
The weather has turned on us
Do not see this
    With cross eyes
Unless it's to then
    See straight culpability
Not only the lambs
But also, bulls
Go to slaughter
Do not hold faith
    In your own will

                    Salem 12.04.18

*

In our relationship
I moved in trust
In slumber
     The breaking of our covenant
Woke me
As a sleeping passenger
Like my spirit moving on
And I awaken in the ride

           Cuba, New Mexico 08.19.22 @1735

*

Is that what this
    Foul-felt fate
    Foreshadows?
Nine out of nine times
I have thoughts of a tenth
Overcast blocks my stars
I gave my heart away
    And there's no return
The void urges
Perpetual spurn
Now relegated to guard

                  Salem 10.29.17 @0433

*

    Crying in the flag
    Cling to the rocks on which
    The torrent tide torments
    In the shallow depths
        Of a deep ocean
    Genocide by dilution
    My mixed ancestry estranges
    I am told to let go
    The hand of my ancestor

                          Newport, OR 07.22.19

*

Euthanasia
More than youth in Asia
We are complicit
Murder of innocents
Murders our innocence

Turn from self-serve tendencies
That divorce within us
When did beauty, joy and comfort
Become not enough?
Never ever enough

                                      Salem 10.01.19

*

You look around here
A place where a many some
Wanted their waning days
Their end sum
The living go to assume
It was ill attributes
Of all this Northwest beauty
Overcast. Fog. Rain.
Ignore Verdancy,
The silver-cast flattering light,
Eyes off the misty mysticism
Divert attention of
    Fresh lung-fulls
Somehow the harmony
Turned discordant
The young turned on the old
They grew old
Then turned on the young
Long addiction
Turned you on yourself

                      Newport, OR 07.22.19

*

What is your relationship
With the eternal?
A footprint
A breath
A particle
A sidenote?
There is a dividing
    Line between

                        Salem 08.01.20

*

While I now walk
As I breathe
I earn your words
Delight in the praise post mortem
That day
When I am gone
When the sun shines down
You know I am there
The chimes in the wind
The brightest star in night

                                        Salem 04.03.20

*

Joyous songs
Beats give reference
To past beats
And tail pitched high
Gloomy
Songs that have beats
Disappear, pitched low

                      Corvallis, OR 10.02.98

*

Life- more often odd
What gives us that impression
More odd than not
That normal defines
Common confines

                              Salem 10.18.20

*

We are just glass panes
Acting profane
Projectiles passing by
Brink of disaster
Kept intact
They have said it all
Including contradiction
So much more to be said

                Christmas Valley, OR 05.09.21

*

God asks of us
Because we can
Accomplish what
    He cannot alone
For He is in us
But is not us
    We are one atoned
Presence can be felt
Not witnessed
Until fulfillment of faith
Eternal rest at home

                              Salem 11.26.17

*

Lessons from the street
See the battles
It is not the most provocative
     Loudest
Definitely not the most popular
Who are victorious

                    Keizer, OR 04.09.17

*

Deed you well
    And dig it deep
My litany of deeds needs growth
My will as deep as the well
I will wish you well
Bid you well
Well-wish my will perseveres

                        Salem 04.12.22 @1909

*

```
1000 miles from Albuquerque
In turn
1000 miles from Umatilla Rez
Pushed away
    In the middle
Ultimately pushed out
I walked away
Subsequently lashed out
Against
```

                    Snowville, UT 08.19.22 @0556

*

Annexation of peace
Anticipating
There is evening in the morn

                          Salem 09.17.17

*

Wind the second's hand
To push the hours

                      Corvallis, OR 06.03.99

*

Euro and buffalo mix
Pair-of-bull, Bi-bull
Makes me bison

                    Salem 04.09.22 @0052

*

The most notorious
     Are still good
By read, not deed
One sided
As negative example to avoid

                    Salem 04.09.22 @1144

*

It is our fate
I see in you
High expectations
In one rendezvous

                        Corvallis, OR 04.02.99

Darkest shadows
Cast by brightest light
Dark, dark
    Foreshadowing

                    Salem 10.15.17

*

Old. Older
Young. Younger
No matter
We are all in the same age
All important
Share matter

                                                          Salem 09.30.21

*

Let us first acknowledge
That we are walking wounded
Then seek healing
Over consolation
Praying out in exhausted breath
Crying out in fear of death
Peaked high hopes
Discovered steep slopes
Struggling to connect cause
Damn lusty filth
Fxxx that temptation
Renders me mere meat

                                        Salem 04.27.20

*

Worrisome
The trillion things
That could go wrong
If our creator was chaos

                              Salem 02.18.19

*

The tolling of the bell
Hear ye, hear ye
Trolling from hell
The death knell
Then the death toll

                                        Salem 05.16.19

*

Feel the gravity stronger
Holding me down
And grounded
    To the
Celestial body
To that, which I am closest
With whom, we share orbit

                              Salem 04.06.22

*

Caught red handed
Blink
I shrink
Back
Yet irreversible

    Ute Mountain, Colorado 08.19.22 @1414

*

There are features
That distinguish
     Part of your identity
There are some
     To change
And/or could change
Then there is that piece
I hope you can accept
On way to opus

> Salem 11.26.17

*

Doubled down on 3
Ended up with 6
Running far from the truth
Down this path
Wonder where truth ever exists
Estranged by distance

                        Salem 11.16.20

*

Strike a chord
Touch a nerve
Follow my word
It caught up to me
Avoid my shield
Fall on my sword

       Albany, OR 06.11.15

*

Every story has its angle
For certain
Every angler has their story

                        Salem 09.11.19

*

Only way for help
You must escape from here

Navajo Reservation, New Mexico 08.19.22
@1514

*

So lonesome
Any attention
Feels like a serenade
When all else fails
You failed yourself
At your lowest
Depressed basin
You can always
Donate remaining energy
Give yourself away to others
Reversal of fortune

                                            Salem 10.02.18

*

Denying my ancestry
Kills my identity
On my Sioux-side
Where do I belong
Estranged and denied
From vast lands of my past
And immediate blood
    In vein

                        Salem 01.26.21 @1241

*

I am tender
I am weak
Tasting exhaustion
I shall sleep

                    Corvallis, OR 02.18.99

*

The future flawed
Because it's made of man
Identity made of
Who, what, when, how, why, where
    We are
And that which we wish
    To be
Disgruntled be the man
Acquainted with his dissonant nature

                          Salem 10.16.15

*

E-V'er Junior
That's who they say I was
Followed every song
Before the roaring buzz
E-V'er Junior
I looked up LegalZoom
E-V'er Junior
Met your legal doom
Took a salt bath
Got into your lungs
That which you endured
Pain and anguish stung
Torn limb to limb
Remains soaking rags
Then you left the office
In a yellow
Ledbetter bag

                                        Salem 08.02.21

*

Bird on a wire
Look, a dove above
Peace on the line
Partitioning two sides of sky

        Christmas Valley, OR 12.11.2021

Artist brushes
With death
To feel
Alive

      Salem 08.16.19

*

Term of art
Nuance vs semantics
Therapy vs creativity
Hypocrisy vs struggle
Pain vs squander
Hapless vs time
Five against versus

                          Turner, OR 08.08.22

*

Striking out
Against the faceless assailant
Based on one
Damning descriptor
Coloring perspective
Hue are wrong
Hear-say heresy

                                              Salem 06.02.15

*

Could you tell?
Fallen to silence
In the back of this hotel
Lost your heart
And that was your guide

                    Salem 07.22.15

*

Prayer powerful
As much the other direction
    In cursing a
    Great name in vain
When bon mot lost on Heaven
One will live like hell

                      Salem 05.21.21

*

It is in my fabric
Do not rush me
To be laid out, full view
Convey the lesson
Be the teacher
    Not the lessen-er
To be Pacific in our aim
From red pipestone
Mission in our direction
Conviction come cascading down

                      Newport, OR 07.11.20

*

```
Freedom-
I will die for my life
Salvation-
I will live for my death
```

        Salem 05.06.21

*

In my arms
I felt your muscle twitch
Erratic breathing
As you dreamed in slumber
It was some years back
    That I ground my teeth
In stressed sleep
In that point of hope
I found the point of hope
Last week
    I lamented the week before
The pressure enabled me
To hear my own blood pulsating
Within my ear
My vitality gave rise to the future

                      Salem 11.22.19

*

Me
I have not eaten
Amen
I emanate me
Nomen
I emulate no poet

                Sand Hallow, ID 08.19.22

*

Children at play
Men at work
Women at love

                Christmas Valley, OR 10.02.21

*

My nomadic Nakota where-house
Pitched on the prairie
Perched on a ledge
Vibrant on the great plains
Moving on, within

                              Salem 10.23.19

*

Put an eye on that
Put an "I" on it
This, right here
Not that, over there
You'll put your "I" out

                                        Salem 10.06.21

*

Surreal disorientation
We are upside down
     In our house
What is wrong?
Exigua got your tongue
This life
Ain't what we anticipated

                    Salem 10.08.21 @0732

*

Sympathize hypocrisy
    As struggle
Rust
Under the paint

                    Corvallis, OR 04.08.99

Water and fire mesmerize alike
Bonfire and surf upon the beach
People in boat
Energy undulating underboard
Focused on self, text and tan
Missing life around
Sea lions right outside our wake
    Eating fish
Miss a lot but
That is their reality
They would say life is dry

                  Newport, OR 11.10.19

*

The truth
Is a straight line
Through pale perceptions
And crooked intentions
Despite circular arguments
Denial of existence
Arrow with a point

                            Salem 06.07.21

*

Best summarized
Verbatim

                Corvallis, OR 05.09.99

*

If not obstinate
Perhaps they were musicians
Maybe poets
Told them to refrain
And they continued
To do it repeatedly

                                                         Salem 02.24.19

*

Revenge, fugitive, resentment
Have no place here
Where our enduring closeness
Dulcet affections
Confections of love
Dominate in our domicile
Former dichotomy
Treasonous as we are adjoined
Take bow now
    For eternity

                      Salem 11.03.19

*

Blackest black
Noir tres noir
Negro intenso
Permian Basin
Underground ocean
Powering the surface
In turn
    Burns into the atomos

                    Amarillo, TX 08.22.22 2355

*

It started
79 Jupiter red eye flight
Search far and wide
Your fingerprints
Like a topographic map
No treasure marked
Perhaps the fountain
    Of youth
Is more like
    Eutrophication

                      Salem 08.18.22 @0921

*

I call their bluff
I call them out
It all ends
    When I call their name

					Salem 02.20.21

*

Life with Brad
Arbiter of truth
In all hope
Hope sometimes reality
Bromides vs Bona Fides

    Christmas Valley, OR 05.20.22 @0021

*

Aging Vitruvian man
Measurement by
Earth, Heaven and hell
Circle triangle square
Attempts to elevate
The spacecraft shot
    Into the stratosphere
Unexpectedly exploding
Continued into the heavens

                        Salem 03.08.19 @0322

*

Live to feed self
Net zero

Live a gross life
Return to the fallow ground
Need to deprive
Yourself
To rebuild good hunger

                        Salem 03.08.19 @1217

*

Walking under rainbows
Swimming past
    Ever-living hydras
Tasting raspberries
    From the center
    Of the universe
Why listen
To simpleton celebrities
1000 mile stare the wrong way
Take real long view
Give me some more, give me
Some more,
    Give me some more oh

                      Salem 06.09.20

*

The severed limbs
Of the mighty oak
Have not
The numerous rings
As the trunk

           Castle Rock, CO 08.24.22 @1059

*

Led into battle
For my country
Old Glory
    Wrap my wounds
Yankton Flag
    Tourniquet

                                  Salem 06.02.22

*

You pigeon-holed yourself
To the hawks
We have superpowers
As humans
We take for granted
Flagrant ways self-serving
To the point
    You lose all meaning
No way to have yourself
    Guaranteed eternity on earth
May try with publication
Progeny wanting substantiation
That others carry on your name

        Christmas Valley, OR 03.11.21

*

Father, son, husband, Holy Ghost
Running through the hail
    Pelting my coat
Tears stream out
Without a cry
Passer-by without an alibi
Those who know me not
Try to define
Now I caught the clarity
Not despite
But through the pain
    Transforming energy
    Fourth rendition
    Giving inspiration
Pulling you along for the ride

                Portland, OR 06.06.22

*

White light
Full spectrum
Demonized for shadow cast
Not everything; your cost
Could be a Pentecost
Not everything you lose
    Is a loss

                       Salem 03.11.21 @1104

*

We deride though
We are the deviants
Act of God or governor?
Lies swilling
Fires burning
Swirling smoke suffocating
Just give me one good reason

                              Salem 09.18.20

*

"Better than nothing"
Superior as something
Or
Inferior to all
Black hole
Superstar in density
Substellar in light

   Ute Mountain Reservation, CO 08.19.22

*

The system confounded
Then restricted us
We decidedly fought,
    Pushed against
When the lid snapped tight
We adjusted to fit
Into the spaces between us
We then realigned priority
To where we've been wronged
Off right

                      Salem 07.29.20 @0308

*

As I stand
Right here
Feel my fate
Objectified by my surround
Rickety sun bleached burnt out barn
Scars on it
Epitaph writ
I should go, not to own
My sum lessened in this aggregate
As I go
Change of fate

                Echo, OR 08.18.22 @2246

*

We are all going
The same direction
It is a certain tide
Before we know it
It is over
Trend vanquished
That is RIP tide
Blind as in prosperity
Deaf as an all-star celebrity
No, the most of us shall push
Against and press forward
Work to fix
    Everything always breaking
Exasperated and traumatized
Yes, press on
Heartily

                          Salem 05.27.22

*

Opt in
Or
Opt out
It is our special position
Opt ion

                       Salem 11.21.21 @2304

*

Focus on the road
Memories indistinct
Watching the end horizon
Distinctive road,
Peripheral blurred
Dedication to truth
    Makes for steadfastness
You do
Or you do not
Gatekeeper

                         Gilchrist, OR 11.29.20

*

Not deserving of a burn down
We all have dead branches
On a living tree
Funeral pyre
Much more than an effigy

                            Salem 12.06.17

*

Worldly things wrought
    From Heaven
Perplexing, Heaven moves
Not worldly
    Antithesis of Heaven
How our celestial particulate
Yearn for above
Away from this
How we confuse worship
    Of worldly things
As celestial endeavor
Mistaken as Heavenly
Nothing inevitable
Two sparks akin
Conjoined inextricably
One a flash, one perpetual

                Salem 06.01.19

*

I am the kind of rare breed
Rarity that could
Love you forever
The hit and the sober
The hit and the classic
The hit and the defense
The hit and the tackle

                Christmas Valley, OR 12.31.20

*

Edge of disaster
Precipice of faith

                      Salem 12.26.20 @1735

*

Desert stripped us
Of our defenses
And our iniquities
We had to provide to our thirst
No peace in the sedate mind
Some set out on a search
You sojourned away from faith
What developments
Have you realized
Nada, only anti-material
There is no alternate Truth
    To discover
Only facets of the One

                                      Salem 02.20.21

*

Various wounds
Can be mortal
If let-left to fester

                    Salem 06.17.22 @0007

*

I get paid accolades
For which I do not
Have pockets

                     Corvallis, OR 03.05.99

*

You have a list of names
    On a page
The darkness of the harm
If I gave you my list
    On that page
It would blot it all out black

Salem 07.31.20

*

Incomplete control
Good by word
Not by deed

      Salem 09.13.22 @1054

*

```
A condition
Defines the stagnant
Publishing would solidify
     The identity
For those wanting change
     Will grow
     And use that
     As a point of no return

     Christmas Valley, OR 10.02.21 @1354
```

*

```
The good word rained down
I sheltered against it
Not accepted as a river
     Water carving a channel
     Flowing life internally
Not as an underground aqueduct
     Quenching the desert
Not as a cleansing shower
No- I deflected with roof
But then reflected with proof
If not mist
Cold dawning
```

                                                  Salem 08.23.20

*

No matter what it was
Or was not
We were meant to
Be there that time
He was meant to
Say it in that way
We were meant to
Hear it that way
You were meant to
Inquire about it
And we were better
     For it
Now it worked out
     Better this way

                              Salem 09.11.22 @1556

*

The cool water cold
Traveling over the mountains
To the streams
And now to me
That water warms in hand
Now warm water
Now the same family

       Christmas Valley, OR 03.21.21 @1029

*

I did not go there
For the education
Not there
I came there for
The increase
Of one degree

                        Salem 07.29.20 @1346

*

The wind is in my favor
The tide is not
The light tilts favorably
The heat, caught in a pot
Building a boiling
Shaking and quaking
Pressure, pressure!
Pressure, pressure!
Made the food
Now I'm fed, led to bed

                                        Salem 07.15.21

*

The beginning of the rainbow
Is light
Suspended droplets
The body is rain

Leaves you
Elusive end of the rainbow
Tales of treasure, unfulfilled
Trails between sunray and moonbeam
Prism, out of angles

           Pleasant Hill, OR 05.19.22 @2006

*

```
Find a creature foreign
Look at those eyes
They are not eyes
They can not-see
Sightless eyespots
Shaken my core
Step back
Not sure
     Of what is navigating
```

                                        Salem 09.15.21 @0729

*

Intently inhale
The fresh air
Deeper than as you had
The smoke

                Gilchrist, OR 08.22.21 @1255

*

Awards and Honors

- October through November 2022- Singular Award, Imitating Imitation Writing Contest; Writer's Café (Of Something Great, Cantus, 2010). Cogito Group; Presented by Swagato Saha

- October through November 2022- Particular Award, Imitating Imitation Writing Contest; Writer's Café (Ability Falls to Will, Cantus, 2010). Cogito Group; Presented by Swagato Saha

- March 2015 — Hero Award, Salem Health; Salem Hospital ICU Medical Social Worker

- January 2015 — Hero Award, Salem Health; Salem Hospital ICU Medical Social Worker

- December 2014 — Team Award, Salem Health; Salem Hospital ICU Medical Social Worker

*

Shadow Catcher
Syzzer
Cornflake
Palaka
B Dizzle
D Train
The Voice
Big Baby
Paco
Chief Iron Stomach
Hatchet Man
Bravo Papa Delta
Chopper
Cali
Brine
Big Hungry
Conan

Publications

- Epiphaneia: Lost Poems of Epistemological Endeavor (2024)
- *Shadow Catching: Poems of Existential Peering (2022)*
- *Syzygy: Poems of Essential Theory (2020)*
- *Dose: Poems of Quintessential Ethereality (2016)*
- *Cantus: A Book of Poems (2010)*

Cantus: A Book of Poems
Paperback ISBN-13: 978-0-982-9733-0-1 & ISBN-10: 0-982-97330-6
Hardcover ISBN: 978-0-982-9733-3-2
Paperback (5x8) ISBN-13: 978-1-966716-00-6 & ISBN-10: 1-966716-00-1
http://www.amazon.com/Cantus-Brad-Dehler/dp/0982973306/

Dose: Poems of Quintessential Ethereality
Paperback ISBN-13: 978-0-982-9733-1-8 & ISBN-10: 0-982-97331-4
Hardcover ISBN: 978-0-982-9733-4-9
Paperback (5x8) ISBN-13: 978-1-966716-01-3 & ISBN-10: 1-966716-01-X
https://www.amazon.com/Dose-Quintessential-Ethereality-Brad-Dehler/dp/0982973314

Syzygy: Poems of Essential Theory
Paperback ISBN-13: 978-0-982-9733-2-5 & ISBN-10: 0-982-97332-2
Hardcover ISBN: 978-0-982-9733-5-6
Paperback (5x8) ISBN-13: 978-1-966716-02-0 & ISBN-10: 1-966716-02-8
https://www.amazon.com/Syzygy-Essential-Theory-Brad-Dehler/dp/0982973322

Shadow Catching: Poems of Existential Peering
Paperback ISBN-13: 978-0-982-9733-6-3 & ISBN-10: 0-982-97336-5
Hardcover ISBN: 978-0-982-9733-7-0
Paperback (5x8) ISBN-13: 978-1-966716-03-7 & ISBN-10: 1-966716-03-6
https://www.amazon.com/Shadow-Catching-Poems-Existential-Peering-Brad-Dehler/dp/B0BMY5M9CN

Epiphaneia: Lost Poems of Epistemological Endeavor
Paperback (5x8) ISBN-13: 978-0-982-9733-8-7 & ISBN-10: 0-9829733-8-1
Hardcover ISBN: 978-0-982-9733-9-4
https://www.amazon.com/Epiphaneia-Lost-Poems-Epistemological-Endeavor/dp/0982973381

NOTES

Thank You

www.ingramcontent.com/pod-product-compliance
Lightning Source LLC
Chambersburg PA
CBHW022054150426
43195CB00008B/129